UNIVERSITY OF NORTH CAROLINA
STUDIES IN THE ROMANCE LANGUAGES
AND LITERATURES

ROMANCE TRENDS IN 7th AND 8th CENTURY LATIN DOCUMENTS

Frieda N. Politzer

and

Robert L. Politzer

Harvard University

THE UNIVERSITY OF NORTH CAROLINA PRESS
CHAPEL HILL

Number Twenty-one   1953

Copyright, 1953
The University of North Carolina Press

PREFATORY REMARKS

Part I of this study presents primarily the results of research undertaken by Frieda N. Politzer, while Parts II and III are the contribution of Robert L. Politzer. However, the authors counterchecked their findings in order to assure the greatest possible accuracy in the results presented here.

The main emphasis in this work is on straight presentation of the factual evidence derived from the statistical examination of the documents. The bibliography and the discussion of the theories of other authors do not claim completeness, but are intended only to give a minimum framework within which the findings are presented. Some important works, such as for instance Hugo Schuchardt's still fundamental Der Vokalismus des Vulgärlateins, do not appear in the bibliography, since their findings have largely been incorporated in other works, and some problems which are raised in the discussion but which are tangential to the main issues have not always been followed up.

In spite of the most careful examination and evaluation of the material, we have shared the experience of others who have presented large scale statistical examinations of language texts, namely that human error and individual interpretation exclude hundred per cent accuracy (see for instance, Hayward Keniston, Spanish Syntax List, New York, 1932, p. 5). The inaccuracy, however, appears to be well within the 5% margin of error--this means that consecutive examinations of the same material never varied by more than 5% from the original count--and therefore the conclusions based on the statistics presented here are in no way invalidated.

The authors wish to express their appreciation to the Stanwood Cockey Lodge Foundation for a grant which has made the publication of their findings possible.

F.N.P. and R.L.P.

TABLE OF CONTENTS

PART I

Dialectal Features in Eighth Century Latin Documents of Italy

- Introduction 1
  - 1. Purpose 1
  - 2. Description of Material 2
  - 3. Method 3
- Phonology 6
  - 1. Accented Vowels 6
    - 1.0 Introductory Note 6
    - 1.1 a, ĕ, Ĭ, ŏ, ū 6
    - 1.2 ē>i, Ĭ>e 7
    - 1.3 ō>u, ŭ>o 7
  - 2. Unaccented Vowels 8
    - 2.0 Introductory Note 8
    - 2.1 ē>i, Ĭ>e 9
    - 2.2 ō>u, ŭ>o 9
    - 2.3 a, ū 10
    - 2.4 ĕ>i 10
    - 2.5 Ĭ>e 10
    - 2.6 ŏ>u 10
    - 2.7 Other vocalic phenomena 11
    - 2.8 Summary 11
  - 3. Consonantal Phenomena 12
    - 3.0 Introductory Note 12
    - 3.1 Simplification, Gemination 12
    - 3.2 Intervocalic Occlusives 13
    - 3.3 Final -t and -s 13
- Noun Declension 14
  - 4. First Declension Singular 15
    - 4.1 Nominative 15
    - 4.2 Genitive 15
    - 4.3 Dative 15
    - 4.4 Accusative 16
    - 4.5 Ablative 16
    - 4.6 Proper Names 16
  - 5. Second Declension Singular 17
    - 5.1 Nominative 17
    - 5.2 Genitive 18
    - 5.3 Dative 18
    - 5.4 Accusative 18
    - 5.5 Ablative 19
    - 5.6 Proper Names . . . .
      - 5.61 Nominative 19
      - 5.62 Genitive 20
      - 5.63 Dative 20
      - 5.64 Accusative 20
      - 5.65 Ablative 21

6. Third Declension Singular 21
   6.1 Nominative 21
   6.2 Genitive 22
   6.3 Dative 22
   6.4 Accusative 22
   6.5 Ablative 23
   6.6 Proper Names 23
7. First Declension Plural 24
   7.1 Nominative 24
   7.2 Genitive and Dative 24
   7.3 Accusative 24
   7.4 Ablative 25
   7.5 Summary 25
8. Second Declension Plural 26
   8.1 Nominative 26
   8.2 Genitive 26
   8.3 Dative 26
   8.4 Accusative 27
   8.5 Ablative 27
   8.6 Summary 27
9. Third Declension Plural 28
   9.1 Nominative 28
   9.2 Genitive 28
   9.3 Dative 28
   9.4 Accusative 29
   9.5 Ablative 29
   9.6 Summary 29

10. Neuter Plural 30
    10.1 Second Declension 30
    10.2 Third Declension 31

Conclusion 33

PART II

On the Origin of French Romance

Introduction 36
   1. Purpose 36
   2. Description of Material 36
Selected Phonological Phenomena 37
   1. Accented Vowels 37
      1.0 Introductory Note 37
      1.1 $\bar{e} > i$, $\breve{i} > e$ 37
      1.2 $\breve{u} > o$, $\bar{o} > u$ 38
   2. Unaccented Vowels 38
      2.0 Introductory Note 38
      2.1 $\bar{e} > i$, $\breve{i} > e$ 38
      2.2 $\bar{o} > u$, $\breve{u} > o$ 39
      2.3 $\breve{e} > i$ 39
      2.4 $\breve{o} > u$ 40
      2.5 $\breve{i} > e$ 40
   3. Consonantal Phenomena 41
      3.0 Introductory Note 41
      3.1 Intervocalic Occlusives 41
      3.2 Simplification and Gemination 41
   4. Summary 42

PART III
Synthesis of Previous Findings by Study of Scribal Habits

1. Purpose and Method 44
2. The Intensification of the Stress Accent in
   Northern France 44
3. Comparison of Habits of Eighth Century
   French and Italian Scribes 46

   Concluding Remarks 49

   Footnotes 51

   Bibliography 56

   Appendix A 58

   Appendix B 62

   Appendix C 66

Part I

DIALECTAL FEATURES IN EIGHTH CENTURY VULGAR LATIN
DOCUMENTS OF ITALY

INTRODUCTION

1. Purpose

The Eighth Century is acknowledged to be an important period in the development of the Romance languages, first because it is the last century before the emergence of a Romance tongue, and secondly because it is the only century of the pre-Romance period from which we have any considerable amount of original material. Various previous studies have been made of Late Latin material, those of M. A. Pei and R. Politzer having dealt exclusively with Eighth Century documents.[1] These latter works concerned themselves principally with an attempt to ascertain the degree of identity between the written and spoken languages of the Eighth Century. However, the study of R. Politzer also included a consideration of dialectization, insofar as it contained a comparison of his findings with those of Pei. This comparison brought out the fact that certain phenomena--particularly changes of unaccented vowels and fall of final consonants--occur with considerably different frequencies in the documents from Northern Italy and Northern France. The difference in frequency was found to be so impressive that a conclusion as to an underlying differentiation between Eighth Century Northern Italian and Northern French speech seemed justified.[2]

It having thus been shown that in the Eighth Century certain dialectal differences existed between the documents of France and Northern Italy, it seems logical to suppose that a study contrasting the documents of Northern Italy and Central Italy will also show significant differences. The purpose of this study will therefore be to discover the nature and extent of dialectal divergences as shown in Eighth Century documents from Northern and Central Italy. Such a study should be of particular value not only for Italian, but for all of Romance linguistics as well, since many linguists consider the dividing line between Northern and Central Italian, namely the so-called Spezia-Rimini line, to be the most fundamental and one of the earliest linguistic boundaries, and such an examination as we propose to make should, among other things, serve to indicate whether or not such a line existed in the Eighth Century.

The theory of the Spezia-Rimini line, of which Prof. von Wartburg is perhaps the foremost protagonist,[3] assumes that at an early date the Spezia-Rimini line divided the Romance world into two distinct dialectal areas: a Western Romance speech area characterized by certain urban, cultural tendencies, which--among others--account especially for the retention of final -s in that area, and an Eastern Romance territory characterized by a more rustic type of Latin, in which final -s is dropped. The concomitant of this retention vs. fall of final -s is plural formation from the Latin nominatives in the Eastern Romance area as opposed to plural formation from a Latin accusative or oblique case in the Western area. The other chief characteristic distinguishing East and West Romance is the voicing of Latin intervocalic unvoiced occlusives in the West vs. their retention as unvoiced in the East. This study will therefore concentrate on these two important dialectal features: retention and fall of -s and plural formation, and the voicing of intervocalic occlusives.

In undertaking this investigation we have accepted the documents as having a definite connection with the spoken language of the time, since we feel that this has been established by previous studies.[4] We shall not, however, here concern ourselves with the question of the degree to which the documents represent the spoken language, since whether the language of the documents *is* the spoken language or merely reflects it, will have no bearing on the significance of our findings. For even if the deviations from Classical Latin found in the language of the documents merely indicate a spoken language apart from that of the documents, the relative frequency of those deviations can still be considered as representative of the development of the spoken language itself.

2. Description of Material

We were fortunate in finding a collection of documents well suited to the type of study we wished to make: The Codice diplomatico longobardo, edited by Luigi Schiaparelli (Vol. I, 1929, Vol. II, 1933). This collection contains all the existing legal documents (carte) "written in Longobard territory during the Longobard reign".[5] Some of the 295 documents in the collection are falsifications, while some others are later copies of no longer existing originals. For the purpose of this study we have included only the original documents plus such copies as were made within the Longobard reign (i.e. before 774), in all 206. The texts of the documents are entirely of a legal nature, dealing with testaments, donations, and commercial transactions of various kinds. The editing of Schiaparelli is notable for its meticulous accuracy, reproducing the texts so exactly as even to indicate every letter of doubtful reading, and the material was therefore of particular value for us.

The table which follows summarizes the most pertinent information about the documents:

Place of Origin	Number of Documents	Dates	Number of Scribes	No. of Lines of Text
Siena	21	736-774	16	793
Pisa	11	720-768 (774)	8	652
Lucca	141	723-774	53	6088
Piacenza	13	721-774	5	544
North of River Po	19	725-773	19	850
Totals	205*		101	8927

*It must be noted that while we mentioned previously that 206 documents were used in this study, the total on the above table is only 205; the other document is a single one from Pistoia which was examined but not included in our statistical summaries throughout, as it is the only one from this particular area, and by itself would add nothing to the overall picture.

It is obvious that the documents from Lucca outweigh by far the total documents from the other four localities; because of this the sample of material we have from Lucca is of course far more significant than any of the others. However, at the same time the example from Lucca is far more affected by the habits of individuals since several of the Luccan scribes have written a few hundred lines apiece, which is in direct contrast to the North Italian documents, no two of which were written by the same individual. But whatever the shortcomings of the material itself, it is the best--as a matter of fact, the only material--available that is suited to a study of this kind, and by making a quantitative analysis of facts, and by basing conclusions not on a single phenomenon but on an entire series of developments, the findings should be valid in spite of the imperfections of the material.

The places mentioned in the first column on the table--and these will on all succeeding tables be given in this same order, arranged from south to north--indicate either that the document was written in this city, or is associated with and preserved in the monastery or archives of this city. Actually many of the documents originated only in the general area of the city rather than in the city itself. For instance, the Piacenza documents originate in Varsi as well as in Piacenza, however a number of the documents coming from both Varsi and Piacenza have been written by the same scribe (Maurace). Many of the documents classified under "Siena" come from the Chiusi area, and some from as far south as Toscanella.

The location "North of the River Po" covers a group of cities scattered throughout a widely extended area: the actual cities included are Verona (1 document), Bergamo (2), Como (6), Milan (3), Novara (1), Pavia (3), Treviso (2), Asti (1). Individually these would not be of much significance, but the fact that they are in the same geographic area justifies grouping them together. It should be mentioned here that 12 of the 22 documents examined by R. Politzer in his study are included in this collection, 11 in the group from Northern Italy and 1 in the group from Piacenza, but the reading of these documents for this study differs somewhat from R. Politzer's earlier reading because Schiaparelli's edition is different from, and we believe superior to, Bonelli's.

To locate the areas from which the documents come with regard to modern Italian dialects, Siena, Pisa and Lucca are in Central Italy, in the region where Tuscan is spoken today, while all of the other documents, including those from Piacenza, are from the Gallo-Italian speaking portion of Northern Italy with the exception of Verona and Treviso, which are in the eastern portion of Northern Italy where Venetian is spoken today. It should be noted here, however, that with regard to consonantism especially, Venetian largely follows the same pattern of development as Gallo-Italian; in vocalism Venetian is somewhat more conservative than Gallo-Italian.[8] However, the Eighth Century documents do not show any particular differences from the other North Italian documents, and it was therefore not thought advisable to consider them separately, particularly since three documents would not have provided a reliable statistical basis for comparison with the rest of the North Italian documents.

With reference to the number of individual scribes, we wish to mention that in each of the three groups of documents from Pisa, Lucca and Northern Italy there is a document--the only one by its particular scribe--which is preserved only in a copy; we therefore have no example of the handwriting of the original scribe in these three instances, and the total number of scribes may therefore be considered to be actually only 98. It should also be mentioned that most of the documents also include a few lines not written by the scribe of the document himself, but appended by the witnesses.

The column headed "Dates" simply gives the year of the earliest and latest document from each locale. In the case of Pisa, the last document is dated by inference only, and may have been written in any year between 768 and 774. This last document should be particularly mentioned, since it is the only one of the collection which is of a distinctly different nature: document No. 295 of Schiaparelli's collection is described as a "breve" and contains simply a list of documents. Since it is not a connected text, the morphological count of endings is completely unbalanced, and because of its length--117 lines-- frequently distorts the picture presented by the various declensions. We have therefore followed the practice of giving the count of a given phenomenon in document 295 individually (with a notation to that effect) in all instances where including it in the total count would be an actual misrepresentation of the state of affairs in the documents. For example, of the 88 separate items listed, 61 are described as cartula: this accounts in large part for the 75 occurrences of first declension nominative singulars in -a. Furthermore, of these 61, 32 are specifically a cartula venditioni--explaining 32 of the 38 occurrences of third declension genitive singulars in -i.

3. Method

Since this does not purport to be an exhaustive study of all phenomena contained in the documents, but only a study of the extent of dialectal development in the Eighth Century, we have confined our examination to those particular phonological features and morphological features which were destined to become the basic dialectal differences between Northern and Central Italian:[7] the vocalic system, intervocalic plosives, simplification and gemination, final consonants, and selected phenomena of the noun morphology, especially the formation of the plural.

The basis used in comparing the frequencies of the purely phonological phenomena is the number of occurrences per hundred lines of text. This seems justified by the fact that the texts throughout deal with the same kind of subject matter, using largely the same type of vocabulary and phraseology. In order to compute percentages it would have been necessary to keep count of every single vowel and consonant in all the 8,927 lines of text--a herculean task which would have required years of labor and would at best have slightly increased the accuracy of our figures, while adding little of value to our findings. However, for noun morphology a complete count was kept and the comparative figures given in percentages.

The tabulation of frequencies is followed by a few examples for the phenomenon under discussion. In order to save space, only a few examples, and only those that imply a deviation from the classical Latin norm, have been given. Furthermore, in the case of the morphological analysis, the only examples included are for phenomena from which significant conclusions are drawn. Thus no examples are given for misuses that are so isolated that they can scarcely be considered significant, but can properly be treated as mistakes apparently unrelated to any contemporary linguistic development.

However, in order to familiarize the reader with the type of material used, and the method employed in examining it, we are reproducing here one typical document, chosen more or less at random. Immediately following we shall also include a reproduction of the file card containing the specific information

ROUGH MAP OF ITALY

INDICATING APPROXIMATELY THE LOCATIONS IN WHICH THE DOCUMENTS ORIGINATED.

Key to Locations
North of the Po

1 Asti
2 Bergamo
3 Como
4 Milan
5 Novara
6 Pavia
7 Treviso
8 Verona

N.B. Note that in referring to the locations "North of the River Po" we have included Asti, which is actually south of the Po, but north of the Tanaro, one of the chief tributaries of the Po.

that was extracted from the document for use in our statistical compilation.

The document reproduced, number 71, is a <u>charta venditionis</u>, concerning a business transaction in which Comacino sells to Oportuno a house, a vineyard and the rest of his possessions in the village of Diano in the territory of Toscanella, for thirty gold pieces. We reproduce it here line by line as it appears on pages 216 and 217 of Volume I of the collection. The editor's markings have the following significance: square brackets enclose restored letters; dots below letters indicate letters which were damaged or difficult to read; oblique lines indicate the end of the line in the manuscript; parentheses are used to enclose that portion of abbreviated words which have been supplied by the editor. Naturally any words or portions of words which appear in parentheses were not included in our count. Document number 71 follows:

```
         In n(omine) d(omi)ni D(e)i salbatoris nostris Iesu Christi.
         reg/nante dominis nostris uiri excell(enti)s(simis) Liutpra/ndu
         et Elprandu regis, anno regni ero(um)/ uicensimo octabo et quinto,
         m(ense) decembrio,/ p(er) ind(ictione) octaba; fel(iciter). Constat
   5     me Rodp(er)tu ma/gistru(m) Cummacinu uindedisse et uindedi
         tiui/ Oportuno u(iro) d(euoto) casa cum uinea, clausura, citina,/
         terra, cultum, incultum, mouilem et inmouilem, omnis/ labore uel
         adquisto, quas auire uisu sum in finis/ istius Tuscanensis. unde
         suscipimus a te pretio pro ipsas/ res meam auri pinsanti sol(edos)
  10     trigenta in prefinito pretio, si/cut inter nos bono animo conueni.et
         ab oernam diem in ta sit/ potestatem ipsas res meam, tam mo-
         bilem quam inmouilem, qua[s] / auire uisu sum in uico Diano
         uel in finibus Tuscanensis, uinden/di, donandi, concanuiandi. et,
         in quod minime credimu, si quoquo/ tempore alius dominu
  15     exieri, qui ipsas res meam omniam suam di/ca esset, aut at nos
         uel heredibus nostris molestatu fuerit,/ et ab uno qemqem
         homine minime defendere potuerimus, in re/ meliorata rem, du-
         plis bonis condicionibus, conponere promitimus./ Qem uiro
         cartula uinditionis Gausualdu u(irum) c(larissimum) notar(ium)
  20     iscriu[ere] / rogauimus. Actum Tuscana, ind(ictione) s(upra)-
         s(crip)ta; fel(iciter)./
             S(i)gn(um)  m(anus)  Rodip(er)to u(iri) h(onesti) uinditoris,
         qui anc cartula fieri rogauit./
             S(i)gn(um)  m(anus)  Itip(er)to u(iri) d(euoti) curatori testis./
  25         S(i)gn(um)  m(anus)  Loponi u(iri) d(euoti) testis./
             S(i)gn(um)  m(anus)  Radicauso u(iri) d(euoti) testis./
           Ego Anzo u(ir) c(larissimus) no(tarius) in anc cartula
         uindicioni rogatus ad Rodip(er)tu/ u(iro) h(onesto) uenditori me
         testis supscripsi./
  30         Ego Gausualdu u(ir) c(larissimus) notar(ius) pos tradita con-/
         pliui et dedit.
```

A reproduction of our file card for document 71 follows. The information on the top line, reading from left to right, is the document number, the year, the place of origin, the scribe, and the number of lines of text. The vertical columns represent the five cases, from left to right nominative, genitive, dative, accusative, ablative, while the horizontal lines provide for the first, second and third declensions (singular and plural), the neuter plurals of the second and third declensions, and the proper names of the first, second and third declensions.

		71	739	Toscanella (nr. Siena)	Gausualdu	30
I	S				a-4	a-10,am-1
	P				as-2,am-3	is-2,as-1,am-1
II	S	us-2,u-5	i-5,is-1		um-1,o-1,N-1	o-13
	P					is-3,i-1
III	S	is-1	is-7,i-3		em-4	e-2,i-1,em-4
	P				is-1	ibus-3,is-4,e-1
N	II					
	III					
Pr. N	I					
	II	u-1	o-3	o-1	u-2	u-3
	III		i-1			

On the reverse side of the card, figures were kept for the changes of accented vowels in free and checked position and in monosyllables, and of unaccented vowels in initial, pretonic-noninitial, atonic penult and final positions; the changes thus recorded include $\breve{e}>i$, $\bar{e}>i$, $\breve{i}>e$, $\bar{i}>e$, $\breve{o}>u$, $\bar{o}>u$, $\breve{u}>o$. Other vowel changes occurred so sporadically that they were noted individually in preference to providing spaces on the card. On the lower half of the card notation was made of fall of final -t and of final -s (not including those already counted in noun morphology), reverse addition of final -s and final -t, voicing and unvoicing of intervocalic occlusives, simplification, gemination, prothesis, syncopation, and other interesting phenomena, such as in this particular document, a fall of intervocalic d. A reproduction of the reverse side of the file card follows:

	Fr.	Ch.	Mon.	In.	Pr.Non.	At. P.	Final	
ĕ								
ē	6	1		5				
ĭ		1			1	1		
ī								
ŏ								
ō			1					
ŭ								

-t>∅ - 4 (exieri, dica)   Simpl. - 1 (promitimus)
-s>∅ - 1 (credimu)   Proth. - 1 (iscriuere)
g + e>c - 1 (vicensimo)   Synco. - (adquisto, ta for tua)
                              -d->∅ (oernam for hodiernam)
-t added - 2
-s added - 1

PHONOLOGY

1. Accented Vowels

1.0 It is generally accepted that by the Eighth Century Classical Latin $\bar{e}$ and $\breve{i}$ had merged in most of the Romance world into one phoneme, as had $\bar{o}$ and $\breve{u}$,[1] and this is corroborated by subsequent development in the Romance languages. Therefore in discussing changes of accented vowels, one must keep in mind that the changes $\bar{e}>i$ and $\breve{i}>e$ actually involve a single phoneme /ẹ/ as opposed to the /ĕ/ and /ī/ of Classical Latin, which remained separate phonemes; also that the changes $\bar{o}>u$ and $\breve{u}>o$ involve the phoneme /ọ/ as opposed to /ŏ/ and /ū/ which likewise remained separate phonemes.

1.1 Those accented vowels of Classical Latin which remained--a, ĕ, ī, ŏ, ū--show little or no change in the documents, i.e. these vowels continue to be written in Classical Latin orthography. The very sporadic instances of change which do occur may easily be due to orthographic mistakes, and have no significance whatever in a statistical comparison.

1.2 The tables below give the figures for the changes $\bar{e}>i$ and $\breve{i}>e$.

$\bar{e}>i$	Free	Checked	Monosyl.	Total	Occurrence per 100 lines
Siena	96	38	21	155	19.7
Pisa	37	7	7	51	7.8
Lucca	413	24	19	456	7.5
Piacenza	13	8	2	23	4.2
North. It.	24	15	1	40	4.7

Examples: <u>rige</u> (97)*, <u>vinditor</u> (174)*, <u>ris</u> (192)*

*The figure given in parentheses after each example refers to the document in which it occurs. This will be so indicated throughout.

$\breve{i}>e$	Free	Checked	Monosyl.	Total	Occurrence per 100 lines
Siena	17	5	-	22	2.8
Pisa	13	1	-	14	2.1
Lucca	78	46	6	130	2.1
Piacenza	28	16	3	47	8.6
North. It.	30	35	1	66	7.7

Examples: <u>menime</u> (144), <u>selva</u> (127), <u>sed</u> (for <u>sit</u>, 291)

It will be immediately observed that the $\bar{e}>i$ change occurs with greatest frequency in the most southerly group of documents, while the $\breve{i}>e$ change is notably more frequent toward the north. In each case the reverse change occurs with correspondingly lower frequency.

The distribution indicates that the /e̩/ phoneme had a more open pronunciation in the north. This conclusion is reached in the following manner:

Classical Latin had four front vowel phonemes, /ĕ/, /ē/, /ĭ/, /ī/, represented orthographically by only two symbols e and i. By the Eighth Century, the differences in length had become differences in quality, and as previously mentioned, the /ē/ and /ĭ/ phonemes had merged, leaving the three phonemes /ę/, /i̩/, and /e̩/ for the original two symbols. The /e̩/ phoneme, however, being from the beginning a merger of two other phonemes, had a certain possible variation of pronunciation and was represented by either of the two symbols, depending largely on the original Classical orthography. However, since the sound of the /e̩/ phoneme was constant in the speech of the individual regardless of which symbol was used in Classical orthography, the scribe would occasionally make orthographic "mistakes" in the direction of the symbol for the stable sound to which his own pronunciation of /e̩/ was nearest.

In interpreting the figures on the foregoing tables, therefore, the degree of deviation from Classical Latin orthography in the direction of a given symbol has been accepted as the indication of the pronunciation of /e̩/ commonly spoken in the particular area.[2]

1.3 The same reasoning may be applied to the evidence of change in the back vowel, since the situation is completely analogous to that of the front vowel. Of the four Classical Latin back vowel phonemes, /ŏ/, /ō/, /ŭ/, /ū/, the /ŏ/ and /ū/ phonemes remained stable, developing into Vulgar Latin /ǫ/ and /u̩/. However, the /ō/ and /ŭ/ phonemes merged into the phoneme /o̩/, which could, as in the case of the front vowel, be pronounced in a variety of ways. The degree of openness or closure with which the /o̩/ phoneme was pronounced determined the type and degree of orthographic variation found in the documents.

Below are the figures for the changes $\bar{\text{o}}$>u and $\breve{\text{u}}$>o:

$\bar{\text{o}}$>u	Free	Checked	Monosyl.	Total	Occurrence per 100 lines
Siena	61	17	9	87	10.9
Pisa	14	4	2	20	3.1
Lucca	155	83	56	294	4.8
Piacenza	32	2	-	34	6.2
North. It.	71	4	7	82	9.6

Examples: nuno (211), curte (175), nus (150)

$\breve{\text{u}}$>o	Free	Checked	Monosyl.	Total	Occurrence per 100 lines
Siena	-	1	-	1	0.13
Pisa	5	1	-	6	0.9
Lucca	37	12	1	50	0.8
Piacenza	4	4	-	8	1.5
North. It.	6	4	-	10	1.3

Examples: nomero (84), secondum (60), sont (111)

The occurrence of the change $\breve{\text{u}}$>o is not frequent enough to be of any great value, nevertheless it is significant that the change occurs somewhat more frequently in the northern and hardly at all in the more southern documents. This generally corresponds to the relative frequency of the $\bar{\text{i}}$>e change and appears to verify the theory that the pronunciation of the vowels in Northern Italy tended to be somewhat more open.

The relative frequency of the $\bar{\text{o}}$>u change does not follow the pattern so nicely. The high ratio of change in the most southerly group of documents is quite in accord with the theory that the proninciation of /o/ was more closed toward the south. However, the fact that the ratio of change in the northern document is also high seems to contradict the assumption of a more open pronunciation in the north. The figures for the $\bar{\text{o}}$>u change in the documents from Piacenza and the region North of the Po therefore require thoughtful examination. It will be noted that the ratio of the occurrence of the change in free to checked position is in the three Central Italian groups of documents approximately 4:1, 3:1, and 2:1, while in the two northern groups the ratio is startlingly high, approximately 16:1 and 18:1. Since in these northern documents the occurrence of the change in checked position is in accordance with the expected pattern, there must be some other reason for the very high frequency of the $\bar{\text{o}}$>u change in free position. Consideration of the subsequent development of long $\bar{\text{o}}$ in the Gallo-Italian dialects brings forth the following explanation: the great frequency of the use of the u symbol for the /o/ phoneme in documents from Northern Italy indicates not a closed pronunciation, but a diphthongization of o>ou, the latter part of which diphthong was identical with the /u/ phoneme, and therefore sometimes led the scribe to use the u symbol to represent the ou sound orthographically. This explanation receives credence from the subsequent developments in the language of Northern Italy.[3]

2. Unaccented Vowels

2.0 An outstanding difference of the present-day dialect of Northern Italy from that of Central Italy is the widespread syncopation of Latin unstressed vowels and fall of Latin final vowels in Gallo-Italian[4] --a characteristic shared by French. The investigation of unaccented vowels presented here is an attempt to discover whether the development of this vocalic pattern was in any way foreshadowed in the Eighth Century Vulgar Latin documents.

The discussion of the unaccented vowels requires a brief preliminary explanation as to the method of counting the change in the final syllable: any changes which may be satisfactorily explained as purely morphological developments, and which in any case would be a hopeless confusion of morphology and phonology, have been excluded from the count of phonological changes and will be discussed later in the sections on noun morphology. Such changes include substitution of o for us and um in the second declension singular, of e for is in the third declension genitive singular, and is for es in the third declension plural.

2.1 The table which follows gives the figures for the occurrence of the changes ē>i and ĭ>e, with the rate of occurrence per hundred lines in parentheses after each figure.

	Initial		Pretonic Uninitial		Atonic Penult
	ē>i	ĭ>e	ē>i	ĭ>e	ĭ>e
Siena	81 (10.2)	3 (0.5)	7 (1.0)	22 (2.9)	28 (3.5)
Pisa	7 (1.1)	2 (0.3)	-	12 (2.0)	18 (2.8)
Lucca	44 (0.7)	65 (1.1)	11 (0.2)	170 (2.6)	204 (3.3)
Piacenza	21 (3.8)	6 (1.1)	-	12 (2.2)	49 (9.0)
North. It.	34 (4.0)	4 (0.5)	-	28 (3.3)	40 (4.7)

Examples: rignante (97), praecipisse (146), vertutem (77), confermatione (235), omnebus (77)

In examining the above table it will be noted that in the Siena documents the relatively high ratio of occurrence of the change ē>i in the initial syllable appears to correspond to the frequency of this same vowel change in the accented position, and thus fits in with the theory of a more closed pronunciation toward the south. However, the documents from Piacenza and Northern Italy also show a relatively higher frequency of this change in initial position, which appears to be in contradiction to the development of the accented vowel in this region. These figures, taken together, may however simply indicate that already in the Eighth Century the development of the front vowel was in accordance with the general Italian tendency toward a more closed pronunciation of the vowel in the initial syllable.[5]

On the other hand, the documents from Northern Italy and especially Piacenza show a relatively high frequency of the change ĭ>e in the atonic penult, which seems to correspond to the development of the accented vowel. However, in considering the general picture of the changes in the two northern groups of documents--especially the relatively higher frequency of ē>i in initial position and ĭ>e in the atonic penult--a logical interpretation might be that there was simply a greater uncertainty with regard to all unaccented vowels due to a stronger stress accent.

No figures have been given for the final syllable, as the changes ē>i and ĭ>e in this position can almost invariably be explained by some morphological analogy, and it is extremely difficult to isolate the morphological from the phonological factor. The most frequent of these changes are of course ĭ>e in the nominative and genitive singular of the third declension, which will be shown in the section on noun morphology, and the change in the second and third person singular of the third conjugation (posuet for posuit, 231), which occurs frequently throughout.

2.2 The table which follows gives the figures for the occurrence of the changes of unaccented ō>u and ŭ>o. Here again the final syllable will not be included, as the phonological and morphological aspects of the change in this position are hopelessly entangled, and the consideration of the problem will therefore be reserved for the section on noun morphology. The occurrence of these changes is so sporadic that rate of occurrence per hundred lines has been computed only for the change in the atonic penult. Figures for the changes of unaccented ō>u and ŭ>o are given below.

	Initial		Pretonic Uninitial		Atonic Penult
	ō>u	ŭ>o	ō>u	ŭ>o	ŭ>o
Siena	9	1	9	2	4 (0.5)
Pisa	4	10	3	6	10 (1.5)
Lucca	58	30	13	5	57 (0.9)
Piacenza	-	9	1	8	61 (11.0)
North. It.	1	8	1	5	49 (5.8)

Examples: cunfermator (61), soposita (56), conpunituri (144), volontate (242), volomus (127).

The occurrence of these changes is too sporadic to warrant drawing conclusions. However, the comparatively frequent change in the atonic penult in the two northern groups of documents requires some comment. It will be noted that these figures seem to correspond to the relatively higher ratio of change of the accented vowel in these same documents; this explanation seems inadequate to account for the ratio of change in the atonic penult, which might also be due to a generally greater uncertainty of pronunciation of unaccented vowels in the north.

2.3 Of the five vowels which remain stable in the accented syllable, a and $\bar{u}$ remain stable also when unaccented. There are a few sporadic occurrences of the change of $a > e$ in the final syllable of first declension nouns, but these will be discussed in the section on noun morphology. The change of $\bar{u} > o$ in the final syllable of fourth declension nouns can be interpreted as a merely morphological phenomenon, due to analogy with the second declension[6] and will not be considered here. A very few sporadic changes of $\bar{u} > o$ occur in initial syllable, namely prodenter for prudenter (documents 94, 125, 133).

2.4 The table below gives the occurrences of the change $\breve{e} > i$ in unaccented syllable, with rate of change per hundred lines for the final syllable.

	Initial	Pret. Uninitial	At. Penult	Final
Siena	-	-	1	0 (0.0)
Pisa	-	-	1	5 (0.7)
Lucca	-	2	3	35 (0.6)
Piacenza	2	-	2	20 (3.7)
North. It.	-	-	2	20 (2.4)

Examples: dicembris (59), consintire (254), quatinus (59), scilicit (29).

It is obvious that the occurrence of this change is too sporadic for explanation, with the exception of final position in the documents from Piacenza and Northern Italy. Here the relatively frequent change of $\breve{e} > i$, which occurs in the pronoun (ipsi for ipse, document 183), the ablative of the third declension (homini for homine, document 70), and the third person singular of second conjugation verbs (habit for habet, document 129) may be due merely to greater uncertainty of the vowels of the final syllable.[7] The most logical explanation seems to be that whenever the scribes were unable to maintain the distinction between closed and open e in unaccented position, open e (< Classical Latin $\breve{e}$) was drawn into the confusion of closed e (< Classical Latin $\bar{e}$) with i.

2.5 The change of $\bar{i} > e$ also occurs sporadically in unaccented syllable. The figures for the occurrence of this change are given in the table below.

	Initial	Pretonic Uninitial	Final
Siena	1	1	5
Pisa	-	-	4
Lucca	13	3	7
Piacenza	4	1	1
North. It.	1	1	6

Examples: fenito (68), indevisa (269), me rectorem ordinare iuberis (272).

The interesting thing about this particular vowel change is that it occurs at all. In the final syllable most of the occurrences of the $\bar{i} > e$ change are in the passive infinitive,[8] and more than half of the 23 instances of the change are uses of fiere for fieri. Instances of the $\bar{i} > e$ change in the third declension singular datives and ablative adjective have not been included, as they properly belong to the noun morphology, where they will be considered later.

2.6 The table below lists the occurrences of the change of unaccented $\breve{o} > u$.

	Initial	Pret. Uninitial	At. Penult	Final
Siena	9	-	-	-
Pisa	6	1	3	-
Lucca	29	2	2	11 (0.2)
Piacenza	7	1	2	16 (2.9)
North. It.	3	3	-	9 (1.1)

Examples: udierna (193), antepuserimus (72), diacunu (45), scriptur (130).

Here again is a change which occurs too sporadically to offer much material for discussion. The figures for the initial syllable may indicate a somewhat more closed pronunciation in initial position, which is in accordance with general Italian development,[9] while the more frequent occurrence in the final syllable generally corresponds to the situation with regard to the ĕ>i change in the final syllable, and may be an indication of a greater uncertainty in the pronunciation of vowels in final position. It is noteworthy that most of the changes of ŏ>u occur in nouns of agent, for example genitur for genitor, No. 29.

The total number of occurrences of changes of the vowels ĕ, ī, ŏ in all unaccented positions is definitely greater toward the north, the changes per 100 lines, from south to north, being 2.2, 3.0, 1.6, 10.3, 5.0.

2.7 The table below is a summary of the occurrences of other vocalic phenomena.

	Prothesis	Apheresis	Syncopation	Haplography
Siena	14	-	8	4
Pisa	9	1	2	3
Lucca	98	18	32	27
Piacenza	1	-	1	1
North. It.	-	2	4	5

Examples: prothesis: istauilem, iscriuere (42); apheresis: scepto for excepto (268), redibus for heredibus (145); syncopation: soldus for solidus (139), stabla for stabula (46); haplography: derent for deberent (160), muero for meruero (114).

All of these phenomena occur too sporadically to be of any significance. It is interesting, however, to observe the almost complete absence of prothesis in the northern documents: the one example from Piacenza is doubtful--inistruens for instruens, No. 271--and might also be classified as anaptyxis.

2.8 To summarize the changes of unaccented vowels, a brief comparison of the occurences of all changes by position in the word gives the following information. In the initial syllable, the change ē>i occurs with greatest regularity (which, as has been previously stated, may indicate a more closed pronunciation of the vowel in the initial syllable), while in the pretonic uninitial syllable the most regularly frequent change is ĭ>e.

In the atonic penult, the ĭ>e and ŭ>o changes are frequent, and it is interesting to observe that the frequency of the changes increases noticeably toward the north, the occurrence of the change ĭ>e per 100 lines, from south to north, being 3.7, 2.8, 3.3, 9.0, 4.7, and that of ŭ>o in the same order, 0.5, 1.5, 0.9, 11.2, 5.7. Another interesting fact is that changes of the vowels which in accented position are very stable--namely ĕ, ī, ŏ--do occur, not very frequently, to be sure, but in all unaccented positions. Furthermore, in the atonic penult we have not only the occurrence of all these vowel changes, but complete substitutions as well; for example in document No. 211, latare occurs for latere, in No. 205, latura for latera (both from latus, lateris), in No. 131, vinduta for vendita, in No. 67, titili for tituli, in No. 295, fibila for fibula, in No. 72, conponumus for conponimus. From the evidence of these vowel changes and substitutions, it seems logical to assume that the atonic penult had become a very weak syllable indeed, and was kept from falling entirely (note that the occurrences of actual syncopation are very few) only by the ever-present force of traditional Latin orthography.

With regard to the final syllable, the significant changes are those which do not occur in the accented syllable, namely ĕ>i, ī>e, ŏ>u. The totals of these three changes per hundred lines of text from south to north are 1, 1.4, 1.5, 6.8, 4.1.

The logical conclusion to be drawn from the evidence presented appears to be that in any given area the amount of confusion in the unaccented vowels is in proportion to the force of the stress accent. Therefore in line with the subsequent development of the language of those regions, the gradation of the figures for occurrence of change (particularly in the atonic penult and final position) from Northern to Central Italy may be accepted as a positive indication that in the Eighth Century the stress accent was stronger in Northern and weaker in Central Italy.

Another conclusion which may be drawn has to do with the fact that the vowels ĕ, ī, ŏ, and even ū, which are completely stable in the accented position, sometimes change when in unaccented position. This fact, coupled with the general occurrence of the ē>i, ī>e, ō>u, ŭ>o changes in all areas, although in different distribution, appears to be quite significant, and may be explained as follows: in unaccented syllables there was a general tendency toward neutralization of the open<>closed opposition in both the back and front vowel phonemes, and this tendency had a definite connection with the force of the stress accent. The evidence of change of ī, ū is really too scant to be of real value, however the mere fact that these vowels do change on occasion may indicate that in unaccented syllables they were sufficiently weakened to be drawn into the confusion between ĕ, ē, ī and ŏ, ō, ŭ.

In the atonic penult, however, the confusion reaches such proportions that it is not unreasonable to assume that in this syllable there remained only a single indefinite vowel phoneme.

These apparent confusions of the Classical Latin vowel system therefore indicate the development of the Vulgar Latin vowel phonemes, which may be diagrammed as follows:

		ī	ĭ	ē	ĕ	ā ă	ŏ	ō	ŭ	ū
Classical Latin										
Vulgar Latin	Accented	i		ẹ	ę	a	ǫ	ọ		u
	Unaccented	(i)		e		a		o		(u)
	Atonic Pen.				indefinite vowel					

This diagram shows the general tendency throughout Northern and Central Italian Late Latin. However, the documents under consideration in this study indicate that the tendency toward reduction of the number of vowel phonemes was definitely stronger in Northern Italy, since the occurrence of changes (especially ĕ>i and ŏ>u) is noticeably more frequent there than in the documents from Central Italy.

3. Consonantal Phenomena

3.0 The consonantal phenomena which have been considered for this study include only those which could be expected to show developments of significance for the question of dialectization, namely simplification, gemination, intervocalic occlusives, and final consonants.[10]

3.1 Simplification and gemination occur very sporadically. The number of occurrences of these phenomena appear on the table below.

	Gemination	Simplification
Siena	8	4
Pisa	5	-
Lucca	26	24
Piacenza	4	1
North. It.	4	15

Examples: inviolauellis for inviolabilis (194), tessaurum for tesaurum (193), tulli for tuli (254), sumu for summus, adjective (268), anus for annus (261), abas for abbas (194).

It should be mentioned that of the 15 instances of simplification in the documents from Northern Italy, 12 occur in document No. 81, all of them in pluperfect verb forms, for example <u>accepiset</u> for <u>accepisset</u>. Otherwise there is nothing of particular importance in the occurrence of these two phenomena, and they do not appear frequently enough to be of any significance.

3.2 The table which follows gives the number of occurrences of voicing and unvoicing of intervocalic occlusives.

	Voicing	Unvoicing
Siena	-	4
Pisa	-	2
Lucca	12 (0.2)	13
Piacenza	-	6
North. It.	88 (10.4)	43

Examples: <u>exeguta</u> (138), <u>finido</u> (119), <u>dogomentum</u> (36), <u>sebe</u> (72 - for <u>saepe</u>), <u>memedipsum</u> (61 - for <u>memet ipsum</u>); <u>rocatus</u> (123), <u>metiaetate</u> (72).

These figures are highly significant. As will be noted by the occurrence per 100 lines mentioned in parentheses, the twelve instances of voicing found in the documents from Lucca are hardly more significant than if there had been none at all. Of the documents from the region north of the River Po, there is only one single document which shows no instance of voicing at all--document No. 48, originally written at Pavia, but recopied by a scribe from Lucca; in considering this document, it is of interest to note that in all other respects it is quite in line with the other documents from Northern Italy, which seems to permit the inference that it was only the voicing which the Luccan scribe felt as a "mistake", and all other deviations from the Classical standard seemed to him perfectly normal and acceptable.

The complete absence of voicing in the documents from Piacenza is a strong argument against the theory of the Spezia-Rimini line as an early dialectal divide, as maintained by many philologists.[11] If there was indeed any line of dialectization in the Eighth Century, it seems much more reasonable to suppose that it was the Po River. The absence of voicing of intervocalic occlusives in Piacenza is also surprising in the light of the evidence of a stronger stress accent, as indicated by the higher frequency of the vocalic changes.

The occurrence of unvoicing is also in general correspondence to that of voicing--sporadic in Siena, Pisa, Lucca, Piacenza, and considerably frequent in Northern Italy, as might be expected as a result of confusion in the pronunciation of the intervocalic occlusives.

3.3 Of the final consonants only -<u>t</u> and -<u>s</u> (exclusive of purely morphological phenomena) have been taken into consideration, since -<u>m</u> had already fallen[12] and other final consonants do not fall frequently enough to be significant. A few sporadic instances of the fall of consonants other than -<u>t</u> and -<u>s</u> are: <u>su</u> (for <u>sub</u>) <u>extimatione</u> (177); <u>de co</u> (for <u>quod</u>) <u>agitur</u> (171); <u>quam abere video</u> (for <u>videor</u>) in <u>Roselle</u> (148); <u>chi</u> (for <u>quid</u> - 111).

The table below shows the loss and also faulty addition of -<u>t</u> and -<u>s</u>. The figures in parentheses represent the rate of occurrence per hundred lines.

	-t falls	-t added	-s falls	-s added
Siena	62 (9.5)	22 (2.8)	24 (3.3)	50 (6.3)
Pisa	23 (3.4)	14 (2.1)	14 (2.1)	21 (3.1)
Lucca	315 (5.0)	87 (1.4)	101 (1.6)	115 (1.8)
Piacenza	11 (2.0)	1 (0.2)	5 (0.9)	11 (2.0)
North. It.	36 (4.2)	7 (0.8)	3 (0.4)	10 (1.2)

Examples: -t falls: tene (125), es, oporte (100); -t added: constat me . . . vendedesset (74), ego . . . deplebit et obtulit (194).
-s falls: superiu (178), fori (280), quesierimu (144); -s added: volo ut habeas ecclesia (157), binderes aut dunares bolueritis (66).

The instances of dropping of -t occur almost exclusively in third person singular verb forms. The distribution seems to indicate that awareness of the final consonant was less clear in Central Italy,[13] and the faulty addition generally corresponds.

The distribution of the fall of -s is particularly striking, since these instances include only those which are purely phonological. The distribution of this phenomenon is perfectly graded from south to north, and the occurrence of faulty addition, which includes substitution of -s in the third person singular of verbs, and the addition of -s in the singular of nouns, again is in correspondence. The discussion of -s in the noun declension, and the theory of the influence of -s on the final vowel[14] will be included in the section on noun morphology.

It must be noted that there is not a single example of fall of -s from a verb form in the documents from Piacenza and the region North of the Po, and this complete retention is in accordance with the late preservation of -s in North Italian.[15]

The general conclusion which may be drawn from this picture of final consonants is that the consciousness of the final consonants was gradually diminishing, and that this impulse was traveling from south to north with no apparent dividing line.

NOUN DECLENSION

The importance of the declensional system for a study of dialectal divergences is chiefly the question of the final -s: since one of the main differences between "Eastern" and "Western" Romance is that Eastern Romance forms the plural by vowel change, while Western Romance forms the plural by the addition of -s, a thorough examination of the plurals of the three major declensions is of primary importance. However, for purposes of thoroughness the entire declensional system has been examined, inasmuch as the final -s also occurs in the singular of the second and third declensions. It was also considered worthwhile to discover whether there was any noteworthy difference between north and central Italy in the development of the one-case system, since French, of course, eventually emerged with a two-case system.

In presenting the evidence derived from the study of the declensional system, each of the three main declensions, singular and plural, plus the proper names and neuter plurals, will be considered individually, case by case, first giving a table showing all occurrences of all endings for each locality, and then discussing the interesting and significant data shown by the table. The endings were counted according to the case required by the Classical Latin construction, i.e., ad beata sancta Maria offerimus (51), is counted as accusative, even though the function in the sentence is dative, since in Classical Latin the preposition ad required the accusative case. The application of the Classical Latin standard is actually of course a somewhat questionable procedure and fairly meaningless for the morphology of the noun after prepositions, since from the Eighth Century Latin point of view a noun after a preposition is the object of a preposition rather than dative, accusative or ablative. It was thought best, however, to adhere to the standard of Classical Latin, since the latter is a rigorous one, and not subject to interpretation. The conclusions drawn in this work are drawn not from the actual application of the Classical standard, but rather from the differences among the documents from the different areas, as revealed by the application of this uniform standard.

The fourth and fifth declensions could not be included in this detailed presentation, as they are represented mainly by the words res, dies, manus and occasionally usus, used in completely stereotyped formulas, as for example signum manus (documents 31, 34, 42, 45, et.al); sexto decimo diae mense dicembrio (59), sub die sexto decimo kalendas abrilis (60), duo decimo dies intrantis kalendas magias (69), etc.; pro ipsa res (84), de ipsa res (87), pro ipsa omnem suprascripta res (89), etc.

4. First Declension Singular

4.1 Nominative

	-a	-am	-(a)e	-as	-o
Siena	51	3	-	2	-
Pisa	39 (75)	4	-	-	-
Lucca	474	31	12	-	1
Piacenza	50	-	-	-	1
North. It.	70	2	-	-	2

Examples: donatio firmam persistat (248); de aliam partem est vineas (184); cases of e are uses of ipse for ipsa: ubi ipse sala positam est (286), which can be explained as confusion of gender.

In the nominative singular of the first declension the -a ending remains stable; the 75 occurrences of -a noted parenthetically are in document No. 295 from Pisa (Cf. Introduction). The instances of the -am ending represent merely faulty addition of -m, due to the fact that in the Eighth Century final -m no longer had any phonological or morphological value.[1] It will be noted that of the other endings which occur sporadically, the two instances of -as are in the southernmost group of documents.

4.2 Genitive

	-(a)e	-a	-am	-i	-is	-o
Siena	27 (90%)	3	-	-	-	-
Pisa	54 (93%)	3	1	1	-	-
Lucca	484 (88%)	62	1	2	1	1
Piacenza	12 (71%)	5	-	-	-	-
North. It.	46 (80%)	10	1	1	-	-

Examples: do . . . omnia res mea mediaetate (144); in . . . predicta Dei eclesia . . . potestatem (267).

The -(a)e ending of the genitive singular of the first declension remains quite stable, particularly in the southernmost group of documents. The tendency for the -a(m) ending to creep into the genitive function is somewhat stronger in the north, perhaps due to the generally greater uncertainty of unstressed vowels. Occurrences of other vowels are too sporadic to warrant discussion.

4.3 Dative

	-(a)e	-a	-am	-as
Siena	-	-	-	-
Pisa	4	3	-	-
Lucca	90	44	-	1
Piacenza	2	2	2	-
North. It.	6	7	-	-

Examples: tibi predicta Dei ecclesia offerrere videor (267).

The tendency observed in the genitive for -a(m) to replace -ae appears somewhat stronger in the dative. From the table above, the dative seems to occur much less frequently than might be expected, judging from the number of occurrences of the other cases. The reason for this is that the analytical dative construction--ad plus oblique--appears frequently in the documents, and in accordance with the method established for counting case endings, these instances appear on the tables as accusatives. The rate of substitution of -a(m) for -ae in both genitive and dative combined is definitely greater in the north, the percentage of substitution (from north to south) being 26%, 39%, 16%, 11%, 10%.

4.4 Accusative

	-am	-a	-ae	-as
Siena	27	103	-	1
Pisa	12	106	-	-
Lucca	372	1070	4	2
Piacenza	4	79	-	2
North. It.	31	43	2	-

Examples: ris me iniudicata non relinquam (248), contra hanc pagina (269).

In the accusative the -am ending is largely replaced by -a, however since the -m had no longer any phonological or morphological meaning, little significance can be attached to the orthographic retention of the -am form. In the documents under consideration the rate of replacement of -am by -a shows no pattern whatever according to geographical distribution.

4.5 Ablative

	-a	-am	-ae	-as	-o
Siena	225	16	1	-	-
Pisa	114	1	-	1	-
Lucca	1573	55	4	-	2
Piacenza	103	-	-	-	-
North. It.	42	6	-	-	1

Examples: de suam portionem (239), de suprascriptam rem (240).

In the ablative there are some instances in which the -am ending is used and these appear to be generally correlated with the rate of retention of -m in the accusative, indicating that in some localities there may have been a somewhat greater awareness of the final -m.

4.6 Proper Names

	Nominative				Genitive			
	-a	-ae	∅	-as	-ae	-a	∅	-i
Siena	2	-	-	-	-	3	-	-
Pisa	14	-	-	1	13	1	-	-
Lucca	75	1	1	-	79	8	1	5
Piacenza	15	-	-	-	19	1	-	-
North. It.	8	-	-	-	12	3	-	-

	Dative			Accusative			Ablative
	-ae	-a	-i	-am	-a	-ae	-a
Siena	-	-	-	-	-	-	-
Pisa	1	-	-	-	7	2	7
Lucca	5	8	1	1	19	-	16
Piacenza	-	-	-	-	6	-	5
North. It.	1	1	-	-	6	-	23

Examples: -a in the genitive and dative: cum infantes eius duo nomine Teudiperga et Teudepert (199); signum manus Anstruda (29); tradere videor tibi Rachiperta relicta qd Ratfuns (191).

Proper names of the first declension do not occur frequently enough to show anything of particular interest or significance. In general, the use of endings in proper names corresponds to that in the general noun, except for the fact that the -am ending occurs in only one single instance. The retention of the -(a)e ending in the genitive and dative seems quite comparable, and indeed in the one instance where there are enough occurrences to warrant a numerical comparison--namely the genitive in the Lucca documents--the rate of retention of -ae in the proper names is 90%, while in the general noun -ae is retained in 88% of all occurrences.

5. Second Declension Singular

5.1 Nominative

	-us	-o	-u	-um	**	-r stem			Neuter		
						-r	-o	-um	-um	-o	-u
Siena	41	5	18	-	36%	4	2	-	12	-	7
Pisa	72	19	5	6	29%	3	-	-	36*	7	-
Lucca	483	131	43	14	28%	48	46	2	337	35	42
Piacenza	28	6	-	-	18%	8	-	-	8	-	-
North. It.	82	14	-	-	15%	4	-	-	29	23	-

** Percentage of replacement of -us by other endings
 * Includes 24 instances in document 295 (Cf. Introduction)

Examples: ego ... aut nullo herede meo (62); ego Autelmu cliricu rogatu ... (100); ego Alpertu munitario ... (281); ego Deusdono presbitero ... (246); tu prior et fermum esse deveas (213).

What is most interesting about the nominative singular of the second declension is the gradation from south to north of the substitution of other endings for -us. It seems obvious that the -us ending had a much more significant connotation in Northern than in Central Italy; indeed, in Northern Italy the -us ending is used exclusively during the first half of the century--in the documents from the region North of the Po the use of -o in the nominative appears first in document No. 119 written in the year 755, and in the documents from Piacenza, the first use of -o occurs in No. 159, in the year 762. In this connection it is also of interest to note that in the neuter, where the -us ending does not enter into the question, the substitution of -o is particularly high in Northern Italy.

It should also be noted that the -u ending is completely absent from the two northern groups of documents.

5.2 Genitive

	-i	-o	-um	-us	-r	-u	-is
Siena	80	25	1	4	4	1	5
Pisa	86	33	-	8	-	-	3
Lucca	1174	279	3	23	5	12	17
Piacenza	46	17	-	-	1	-	-
North. It.	112	31	-	3	-	-	-

Examples: signum manus Arnicaus germano ipsius consentientis (77); auris (for auri) soledus numero decem (87); signum manus Bonari filius Auradi (87).

In the genitive the -i ending is largely retained to about the same degree throughout, the percentage of retention, from south to north, being 75%, 72%, 79%, 73%, 78%. Replacement of -i is chiefly by the -o ending, which is not surprising, in view of the fact that -o eventually became the general ending of masculine nouns.

It should be noted that the sporadic uses of the -is ending are all in the three southern groups of documents, and this may be connected with general uncertainty regarding the final -s.

5.3 Dative

	-o	-um	-i	-us	-e	-r
Siena	7	-	-	-	-	-
Pisa	16	-	-	2	-	-
Lucca	273	26	25	13	7	2
Piacenza	12	-	-	-	-	-
North. It.	15	-	-	-	-	-

Examples: tibi ... presbiteri vel ad successori tuo (84); res illa quem mihi et Alperti generi mei obvinet (250).

The normal -o ending is generally retained in the dative. The possibility of the substitution of other endings is shown by the examples from Lucca. The fact that these substitutions do not occur more generally is not particularly significant, since the mere fact that the amount of material from Lucca is approximately ten times as voluminous (Cf. Introduction) as that from any other single locality may be enough to account for the occurrence of the greater variety of endings. To be even more explicit, if other endings did occur in the documents from the other localities in the same proportion as in Lucca, at best there would be only one or two.

It is interesting to note that the -i ending occurs in the dative--perhaps under the influence of the genitive, or perhaps by analogy with the third declension.

5.4 Accusative

	-um	-o	-u	-us	-r	-i
Siena	58	52	19	6	2	-
Pisa	21	36	10	7	-	-
Lucca	318	534	8	30	5	1
Piacenza	28	39	-	1	1	-
North. It.	49	92	-	1	-	-

Examples: recepe ... pretum placitu (288); inter campu et silva (146); per misso suo (233); constat me praenominatus ... vendidisse (174); confirmo locus ipso (100).

The -um ending of the accusative is replaced by -o in more than 50% of all instances except in Siena; however, by combining the total of the -o and -u endings, the -um is outweighed throughout. It should be noted that the -u ending occurs only in the three groups of documents from Central Italy, as does the -us, with the exception of two sporadic instances, one in Piacenza, and one in the North Italian group of documents.

5.5 Ablative

	-o	-um	-u	-us	-r
Siena	211	18	10	7	-
Pisa	118	11	3	10	4
Lucca	2206	262	19	20	17
Piacenza	114	11	-	-	-
North. It.	265	12	-	4	2

Examples: in mediu locu (92); pro anime meae remedium (205); mense februariu (150); neque a me neque a posterus meus posset disrumpi (42).

The normal -o ending remains stable also in the ablative, with occasional substitution of the -u(m) variant. Here again, as in the nominative and accusative, the -u ending appears only in the three southernmost groups of documents, and the -us ending appears chiefly toward the south.

To summarize briefly the significant evidence drawn from the examination of the second declension singular: the frequency of the -us ending in the nominative is diminishing more rapidly in the south, accompanied by a tendency to use -us incorrectly in other cases than the nominative. Further, the -u ending is confined exclusively to the three southernmost groups of documents.

5.6 Proper names of the second declension

5.61 Nominative

	-us	-o	-u	*	-i	**	∅	***
Siena	35	10	16	43%	13	18%	27	27%
Pisa	22	17	9	53%	4	8%	28	35%
Lucca	207	132	98	53%	20	4%	189	29%
Piacenza	11	13	-	54%	-	-	26	52%
North. It.	28	7	1	22%	1	-	35	49%

* Percentage of replacement of -us by -o and -u.
** Percentage of substitution of -i of all forms with endings.
*** Percentage of total in which no declensional ending is used.

Examples: tu suprascripto Lupo (144); ego Antelmo cl. rogatus (205); ego Teudimari... subscripsi (185); ego Chiserat... visum sum (80).

In the nominative of proper names of the second declension the tendency to replace -us by -o or -u is noticeably greater in the three groups of documents from Central Italy and also in Piacenza. The use of the -i ending in the nominative function exists almost exclusively in Central Italy and is obviously strongest in the southernmost group of documents.

On the other hand, use of no inflectional ending is definitely more prevalent in the two northern groups of documents.

5.62 Genitive

	-i	*	-o	-u	-us	-e	-os	∅	**
Siena	37	36%	51	-	-	-	3	14	13%
Pisa	57	60%	15	1	1	-	-	21	22%
Lucca	875	66%	33	20	2	5	-	386	29%
Piacenza	46	54%	21	-	1	-	-	21	24%
North. It.	37	70%	16	-	-	-	-	34	40%

*Percentage of retention of -i of total genitives with declensional ending.
**Percentage of use of no declensional ending of total genitives.

Examples: signum manus Fussiano (66); signum manus Baroncellu (84); signum manus Aduald (253); bersura Lupolos (66).

The replacement of the -i ending in the genitive shows no particular pattern, the -i being largely retained. However, the frequency of the occurrence of -i in the Siena documents seems surprisingly low, especially in view of the more frequent use of -i in the nominative in these same documents.

As in the nominative, the use of no inflectional ending in the genitive is highest in Northern Italy, although this is not the case in Piacenza. Note the reverse addition of -s on three instances in Siena.

5.63 Dative

	-o	-i	-u	-us	-e	∅
Siena	28	13	2	2	-	7
Pisa	1	3	-	-	-	1
Lucca	96	27	2	5	15	61
Piacenza	1	12	-	-	-	1
North. It.	1	1	-	1	-	3

Examples: -i in the dative: res meas offerre Deo et beati sancti Quirici (77); tibi danno Vaalprand episcopo (99).

The use of endings in the dative of proper names does not appear to show anything of significance, nor does it seem to follow any pattern. The relatively high occurrence of -i in Piacenza (note that use of -i in the nominative occurred almost exclusively in the Central Italian documents) might be due to analogy with the third declension, since the dative case is the only one in which the third declension has a long -i.

5.64 Accusative

	-o	-um	-u	-i	-us	-e	∅
Siena	4	-	7	3	3	-	3
Pisa	5	-	13	2	-	-	11 (35)
Lucca	68	47	24	3	16	3	71
Piacenza	3	-	-	-	-	-	1
North. It.	8	-	-	-	-	-	5

Examples: constat me Causulu . . . vendedissit (87); constat me Teudimari . . . vindedisse (185); Teutfrid notaris escrivere rogavimus (88); Vualipertus cl. scribere rogavi (184).

In the accusative the -o ending and the use of no inflectional ending occur with comparable frequency, with the exception of the 35 instances of no declensional ending noted parenthetically in Pisa, which occur in document No. 295 (Cf. Introduction). Note that in the accusative the -u and -i endings again occur exclusively in the three Central Italian groups of documents.

5.65 Ablative

	-o	-us	-u	-i	-e	-um	∅	*
Siena	17	9	9	3	-	-	18	32%
Pisa	25	2	4	9	-	1	38	48%
Lucca	219	16	70	16	1	-	198	38%
Piacenza	10	1	-	1	1	-	20	61%
North. It.	23	2	1	1	-	-	35	56%

* Percentage of total ablatives in which no ending occurs.

Examples: rogatus ad Arnolfu (141); rogatus a Gausfridi (221); rogatus a Gausfrid (221); rogatus et petitus ad Onastasius (288).

In the ablative the -o ending and the use of no inflectional ending again occur with more or less comparable frequency, however the use of no ending is generally greater in the two northern groups of documents. Once again the occurrence of the -us, -u, and -i endings is confined mainly to the three central groups of documents.

To summarize the developments with regard to proper names of the second declension, two main differences from the general noun and three similarities with the general noun should be quite explicitly stated. The two great differences are: (1) the widespread use of the proper name without inflectional ending, which however appears somewhat more frequently in the north; (2) the extension of the -i ending with proper names to all cases, especially in Central Italy, which is probably the explanation for the many present-day Italian names ending in -i.[2] The similarities with the general noun are: (1) the general stability of -us in the nominative, which is particularly strong in the north, although in the general noun the usage in Piacenza compares with Northern Italy, while in the proper names the comparison is with Central Italy; (2) the use of -us for -o and -um, which could be described as incorrect addition of -s, is more frequent in the more southern documents; (3) the use of the -u ending occurs chiefly in the south, with very few exceptions.

6. Third Declension Singular

6.1 Nominative

	Consonant stem			i stem		
	Nom.	-e(m)	%-e(m)	-is,-es	-e(m)	%-e(m)
Siena	40	4	9%	29	7	19%
Pisa	23	6	20%	7	1	13%
Lucca	252	189	43%	107	52	33%
Piacenza	22	17	44%	6	6	50%
North. It.	35	22	38%	22	4	16%

Examples: mediaetatem sit in potestate nostra (200); offersionem firma et stabile valeas permanire (269); ipse Atripert nepote meo ... de seculo recesserit (186).

On the above table the three columns on the left represent the imparisyllabic nouns of the third declension of the type rex, regis, while the three right columns include the civis, civis type of nouns. In both types the normal nominative is still strong. The substitution of -e(m) as listed in the column on the extreme right may, however, represent a fall of -s, but this does not occur according to any pattern, and indeed, in this particular case the morphological and phonological factors are so involved that little significance can be attributed to the fall of -s as a phonological phenomenon.

6.2 Genitive

	-is	-es	-i	-e	-em	Nom.	*
Siena	81	4	27	16	1	-	66%
Pisa	72 (14)	-	22 (38)	3	1	2	73%
Lucca	582	11	194	27	5	11	72%
Piacenza	81	6	9	5	1	6	85%
North. It.	83	20	22	8	1	2	77%

* Percentage retention of -s

Examples: signum manus Aiolfo filio eius consentiente; signum manus Fabrulo filio eius consentientes; signum manus Arnolfo v(iri) h(onesti) et vinditori (141); signum manus Bonari . . . filius qd Auradi homo Pisanus (87); prope muro civitate ista Lucense (127); in hac pacina totalium seu confermatio (73); volumptate patri et matri (194).

In the genitive the preservation of the form with final -s is somewhat higher toward the north. The figures given parenthetically for Pisa refer to document No. 295 (Cf. Introduction) in which there are 38 instances of fixed formulas such as cartula venditioni which occurs 32 separate times in the document, cartula donationi, etc., accounting for the seemingly disproportionate number of genitives in -i which occur in this document.

6.3 Dative

	-i	-e(m)	Nom.	-is
Siena	5	-	1	2
Pisa	4	-	-	-
Lucca	33	16	9	1
Piacenza	18	-	-	-
North. It.	8	-	-	-

Examples: dulcessimo et amavile nepote meo Atripert (186).

Occurrences of the dative are too few to indicate anything other than the apparent stability of the -i ending. Again the larger sample from Lucca, however, shows the possibility of using other endings.

6.4 Accusative

	-em	-e	Nom.	Neut.	-i	-is
Siena	22	23	4	6	-	-
Pisa	16	20	9	7	-	-
Lucca	291	357	29	49	1	2
Piacenza	13	22	1	5	-	1
North. It.	36	33	5	8	-	-

Examples: use of -e: mediaetate reddere debeas (273); use of Nom.: qui necdum claritas oculis haventem (100); ad eius agnitio superimponere (284).

The accusative shows nothing of importance for the purpose of this study. Neither the nominative nor the form in -s, which might have shown interesting differences in frequency, occur frequently enough to be of significance.

6.5 Ablative

	-e	-em	Nom.	Neut.	-is	-i	-es	Adjective -i	-e(m)
Siena	139	51	6	4	2	2	-	9	13
Pisa	85	20	6	1	-	-	-	9	9
Lucca	971	230	25	8	1	3	1	119	104
Piacenza	73	23	4	-	1	-	-	7	2
North. It.	170	36	5	-	-	-	-	24	15

Examples: a nullo hominem (61); sine omnem impedimento (73); pro perennem securitatem (137); me praesente (abl.abs., 137); die octabo de mensis magio (284); da qualibet homini (80); in proprietas nostra (138).

In the ablative there again appears nothing significant. The replacement of -i by -e(m) in the ablative adjective is probably a morphological rather than a phonological phenomenon.

6.6 Proper names of the third declension

	Nominative				Genitive				Dative	
	Nom.	-is	-e	-i	-is	-i	-e	Nom.	-i	Nom.
Siena	8	-	2	-	2	27	-	1	2	-
Pisa	4	3	-	-	6	14	-	4	5	-
Lucca	19	7	1	21	10	67	5	1	7	1
Piacenza	-	3	8	9	1	37	-	1	2	-
North. It.	5	10	3	3	7	49	-	1	8	-

	Accusative					Ablative				
	-em	-e	-is	-i	Nom.	-e	Nom.	-i	-is	-em
Siena	-	3	-	-	-	6	-	1	-	1
Pisa	1	-	-	2	-	2	1	4	-	-
Lucca	1	2	1	6	5	8	2	11	2	-
Piacenza	1	1	-	-	-	11	-	-	-	-
North. It.	5	7	-	-	2	21	2	1	-	3

Examples: -i in the genitive: signum manus Iuhanni (184); signum manus Deusdoni (146); -i in other cases: Nominative: ego Petronaci (100); ubi Leonaci abba preesse videtur (125); Accusative: precepto ... facto in Iohannaci (295); Ablative: rogatu a Petronaci (100); da Iohanni (295).

There are two important points to be brought out with regard to the proper names of the third declension. First, in the genitive the ending -i is already quite generalized, and -is is retained in a very small number of instances, which is in sharp contrast to the high retention of -is in the genitive of the general noun. Second, the use of the -i ending is creeping also into the nominative, accusative and ablative, probably under the influence of the proper names of the second declension.

7. First Declension Plural

7.1 Nominative

	-ae	-as	-a	-is	-es
Siena	1	9	5	-	-
Pisa	3	2	-	-	-
Lucca	31	32	11	8	1
Piacenza	3	11	1	-	-
North. It.	4	12	1	3	-

Examples: dum patrocinias ipsas ... reconditas et intromissas fuisset (127); ... id est ... ancillas, ... vineis ... silvis (56); res illas qui ... mihi obvinet ... tam cases, terra, vinea, etc. (73); duas cartulas ... fuerunt conscriptas (113).

In the nominative plural of the first declension the -as ending is used somewhat more frequently than -ae throughout. The -a ending (with fall of -s) occurs chiefly in the Central Italian documents.

7.2 Genitive and Dative

	Genitive						Dative	
	-arum	-as	-a	-is	-ae	-i	-is	-a
Siena	-	-	-	-	-	-	-	-
Pisa	3	-	-	-	-	-	-	-
Lucca	11	1	1	3	4	1	2	-
Piacenza	1	-	-	-	-	-	-	-
North. It.	6	-	-	-	-	-	-	2

Examples: de suprascripta eclesie rectoribus (131 - referring to two churches); neglegentia usui sui manibus (131); mediaetate rebus meis (165).

The genitive and dative occur too infrequently to show anything of interest. In the genitive -arum remains stable, with sporadic occurrences of other endings in the larger sample from Lucca.

7.3 Accusative

	-as	-a	-is	-(a)e	-i	-arum
Siena	29	9	10	5	-	-
Pisa	20	5	-	2	-	-
Lucca	445	49	23	29	3	1
Piacenza	41	1	2	-	-	-
North. It.	53	3	-	1	-	-

Examples: duas pagine iscrive rogavimus (280); tradedit ... duas petiole (106); duas pagina ... conscripte scrivere rogavimus (139); ad ipse case pertinente (287); ipsi tres petras ... autferere visus sum (118).

The -as ending is generally stable in the accusative, however -a (with fall of -s) occurs with considerably greater frequency in the Central Italian documents. It is interesting to note that -ae occurs almost exclusively in Central Italy and that instances of the use of other endings are also more frequent toward the south.

7.4 Ablative

	-is	-as	-a	-ae	-i	-arum
Siena	26	8	2	1	1	-
Pisa	10	33	5	-	1	-
Lucca	258	99	21	28	5	2
Piacenza	13	16	-	-	-	-
North. It.	30	20	1	-	-	-

Examples: de nostras personas (127); de casas (287); pro terre (113); de suprascripte ecclesiae (143); de rebus mei (136); de suprascripta res meas (73); pro suprascriptas vineas et terra (80); de vineas tua (80).

In the ablative there is a strong tendency for -is to be replaced by -as. The -a (with fall of -s) ending is generally confined to the Central Italian documents, as are sporadic occurrences of other endings.

7.5 Summary: Distribution of -as and -a in all cases

	-as	-a	%
Siena	46	16	26%
Pisa	40	10	20%
Lucca	577	82	13%
Piacenza	68	2	3%
North. It.	85	4	5%

The above table shows the total number of occurrences of -as and -a in all cases of the first declension plural, with the percentage of fall of -s. This may be considered as a purely phonological phenomenon, and it is obvious that the occurrence is almost completely gradated from south to north, although there is a definite break between the Central and Northern documents.

There are two instances of the -es ending--one occurrence of the form cases in the nominative (No. 73 from Lucca) and the place name Cellules (No. 66 from Siena)--which might be cited as evidence in support of the theory of the closing influence of final -s on the preceding vowel; however two isolated examples seem hardly sufficient evidence on which to base an argument.[3]

While the -as ending is most generally used throughout the documents, there are some interesting and significant facts which must be brought out in connection with the use of the -ae ending. The -ae ending occurs with greater frequency in the Central documents--there are only 8 instances of -ae in the two northern groups of documents (Cf. foregoing tables). In the first half of the century, the occurrence of -ae is sporadic in the south (10 out of a total of 104 instances), nonexistent in the north: the first instance of -ae in northern Italy is in document No. 216, in the year 762, and in Piacenza in document No. 249, in the year 770. This indicates that in the Eighth Century the -ae ending was being reintroduced from the south, to preserve the plural connotation, which was in process of being blurred by the fall of -s from the -as plural ending.[4]

The -is ending appears in all cases, and there are even sporadic occurrences of -i, which seems to indicate that the feminine plurals in -i in Old Italian are actually survivals of the ablative ending in -is.[5] However there are also occurrences of place names in -e--Interacchule (No. 178) and Trecase (No. 147), both from Lucca--which survive in Modern Italian with the -i ending--Antraccholi, Tricasi--indicating that -i<-e was an alternative possibility in the feminine plurals, and generally corresponding with the theory of the alternative development of front vowels in the final syllable.[6]

8. Second Declension Plural

8.1 Nominative

	-i	-is	-os	-us	-o
Siena	24	31	8	13	-
Pisa	14	8	-	5	-
Lucca	112	45	15	20	4
Piacenza	11	20	-	-	-
North. It.	26	13	-	1	-

Examples: in loco qua natis sumus (16); servos vero vel ancillas seu aldiones meos ... sint omnes in potestate suprascripte eclesiae (175); ego aut meus heredis; ego ... heredi meus (87); qui de uno germine sunt procreatos (138); conponamus nos ... vel heredis nostro (134).

In the nominative plural of the second declension, -i and -is appear with comparable frequency, but with no apparent pattern in the geographical distribution. The substitution of -os, -us in the nominative seems to be confined chiefly to the Central Italian documents.

8.2 Genitive

	-orum	-is	-i	-os	-us	-o
Siena	2	3	-	1	-	-
Pisa	11	2	-	-	-	-
Lucca	72	5	8	-	1	1
Piacenza	4	3	-	-	-	-
North. It.	14	6	-	-	-	-

Examples: cum consenso et voluntatem filiis vel generis meis (141); in terra vestra q(ui) s(upra) germani (177).

The genitive shows the -orum ending remaining stable, and it is significant of the general trend toward an -i(s) plural that it is the -is ending which is creeping into general use.

8.3 Dative

	-is	-i	-os	-us	-orum
Siena	5	-	1	4	-
Pisa	4	-	2	1	1
Lucca	38	5	1	-	-
Piacenza	2	-	-	-	-
North. It.	7	-	-	-	-

Examples: vendidi vobis ... germani filii qd Petti (177); vobis ... filios et fratris eius (66); defendere potuero ... tuos heredis (dat. of interest) ipsa s(upra)s(cripta) terrula (46).

In the dative -is remains stable, being replaced by other endings only in sporadic instances.

8.4 Accusative

	-os	-us	-is	-i	*	-o
Siena	17	4	16	11	54%	2
Pisa	5	2	4	7	61%	-
Lucca	98	45	64	50	44%	-
Piacenza	4	3	10	3	65%	-
North. It.	27	18	11	-	20%	-

* Percentage -is, -i of total -is, -i, -os, -us.

Examples: potestate ipsi homenis liveros absolvendi (175); que ad me vel duis germani mei pertinet (87); suscepi soledus . . . numero decem (87); tibi vel ad successoris tuo (87); tivi . . . vel ad posterusque supcessoris tui . . . vel ad posterosque supcessori tuo (144); olibi . . . vindedit (288); inter me et filiis meis (16).

In the accusative the -os, -us ending appears to be giving way to -is, -i, and it is interesting to note that the use of the -i ending is confined almost exclusively to the Central Italian documents--the three instances of -i in Piacenza occur quite late in the century, in document No. 248 from the year 770. There appears to be a definite break in the tendency to use -i, -is, occurring between Piacenza and Northern Italy.

8.5 Ablative

	-is	-i	-os	-us	-o
Siena	24	15	5	6	-
Pisa	5	1	7	-	-
Lucca	154	79	36	28	3
Piacenza	13	18	-	2	-
North. It.	31	6	6	3	-

Examples: da germani, de filii vero masculini (127); de posterus tuo (80); cum meus heredis (80).

In the ablative, -is, -i are the predominant endings, with the -is ending remaining noticeably more stable in the one group of documents from Northern Italy.

8.6 Summary: Distribution of -is, -i

	-is	-i	%
Siena	48	36	43%
Pisa	15	8	35%
Lucca	261	142	36%
Piacenza	28	21	41%
North. It.	55	6	10%

The above table includes all occurrences of -is and -i in the genitive, dative, accusative and ablative, and is an attempt to assess the value of the final -s in the -is ending. The percentage of use of -i shows that everywhere but in the region north of the Po the -s had fallen in a large proportion of instances. It is also of interest to note that of the six instances of the use of -i in Northern Italy, five definitely occur in the latter half of the Century, and the one other appears in document No. 81, which in this edition is dated 721-744, but has been dated much later by other authorities.[7]

In general it may be said that as a result of the growing uncertainty with regard to final -s, especially in Central Italy, the -i, -is ending was becoming generalized in order to maintain plural connotation. Between Piacenza and Northern Italy there seems to be a definite break in the tendency to replace -us, -os in the accusative, as well as the fall of -s from the -is plural--indeed it may be said that the documents from the region north of the Po do not follow the others in the development of these two phenomena. The -us ending is actually a variant of -os, perhaps as a result of the confusion between o and u (Cf. Paragraph 2.2), perhaps because of the closing influence of final -s (Cf. Paragraph 7.5).[8]

9. Third Declension Plural

9.1 Nominative

	-es	-is	-ibus	-i	-e	-em	-ium
Siena	5	17	5	2	-	-	1
Pisa	10	2	4	2	1	-	-
Lucca	44	48	14	3	1	4	-
Piacenza	3	12	-	-	-	-	-
North. It.	12	8	-	-	1	-	-

Examples: nos vendituris aut nostris heredis (66); promettemus nusq(ui) s(upra) vendituri (49); possedeas tu tuisque vel heredibus tui (45).

In the nominative plural of the third declension, the distribution of -es and -is follows no pattern and seems to indicate that the endings were completely interchangeable. Note that the ending -i, which is the one destined to survive, appears only in the three Central Italian groups of documents.

9.2 Genitive

	-ium	-es	-is	-ibus	-i
Siena	5	-	-	2	1
Pisa	5	-	-	1	-
Lucca	46	2	3	6	-
Piacenza	4	1	2	1	-
North. It.	17	1	-	6	-

Examples: Terre ipsorum homenis (113); in presentia testibus (87); in ipsorum sacerdoti dominio (171); tua vel heredibus tuis potestatem (49); una cum volontate Gausualdo, Perideo et Facchisi conditori (referring to all three) de ipso monasterio (55).

In the genitive, -ium seems to remain quite stable, with sporadic occurrences of other endings.

9.3 Dative

	-ibus	-es	-is	-i	-ium
Siena	7	-	5	-	-
Pisa	3	-	2	-	-
Lucca	40	2	3	2	1
Piacenza	-	1	1	-	-
North. It.	10	3	-	-	-

Examples: vobis q(ui) s(upra) emtoris (66); testis a me rogitis obtulit (184); licentiam non haveas alii homeni vendere nec donare (261).

The dative retains the traditional -ibus ending in a majority of instances, although -is seems to be coming into general use toward the south. However, the occurrences of the dative are not frequent enough to be significant.

9.4 Accusative

	-es	-is	-ibus	-i	-e	-ium
Siena	7	25	6	7	-	-
Pisa	4	4	3	2	1	-
Lucca	60	63	31	6	2	1
Piacenza	3	10	6	-	1	-
North. It.	14	12	6	1	1	-

Examples: contradidi . . . tres parti (87); quibus emturib(us) aut heredib(us) vestri . . . compellaveris (97); ad subcessori tui conpunituri promittimus (288); per alii homeni (254).

In the accusative, the endings -es and -is follow no pattern, and appear to be used completely interchangeably, as was noted in the nominative case. The ending -ibus appears occasionally and with some regularity, while the instances of the fall of -s are confined mainly to the three southernmost groups of documents.

9.5 Ablative

	-ibus	-is	-es	-i	-e	-e*	-em
Siena	32	26	10	2	1	2	-
Pisa	10	3	4	1	-	2	-
Lucca	232	64	50	5	20	69	3
Piacenza	16	16	2	-	2	5	-
North. It.	19	6	16	-	1	4	-

* This is counted separately, as it occurs in the fixed formula regnante . . . regibus, the dots representing the names of two kings; the word probably no longer had plural connotation.

Examples: da duas partes (129); quis de frates nostros (100); quis de heridis suscessoris meis (269); de ali parte (184); de ordini longi (161); de parenti tui (287); cum omnia res ad ipsa casa pertinente (287).

In the ablative, replacement of -ibus seems well under way, since the combined number of occurrences of -is, -es and their variants without -s is greater than the number of occurrences of -ibus, except in Lucca where the number of instances of -ibus is still somewhat higher.

9.6 Summary: Distribution of -es, -is, -i

	-es	-is	-i	%-i	-e*	%-i+-e
Siena	22	73	12	11%	1	12%
Pisa	18	11	5	15%	2	19%
Lucca	158	181	26	7%	26	12%
Piacenza	10	41	-	-	3	5%
North. It.	46	26	1	1.5%	3	5%

* regnante (Cf. Paragraph 9.5) not included.

The above table is an attempt to discover whether the use of the plural form without -s followed any geographical pattern. It will be immediately observed that forms without -s occur with considerably greater frequency to the south, both in the use of the -i ending and in the total use of -i and -e combined. The column giving occurrences of the use of -e in the third declension plural was included with some hesitancy, since the validity of some of the forms might be argued: as noted on the table, the previously mentioned regnante . . . regibus has been omitted entirely, however other forms in -e appearing in similar constructions, as for instance mecum stante idoneis homenis (No. 81) have been included, since they cannot be put in the category of "fixed formulas"; it is quite possible, however, that by the Eighth Century there was no longer any necessity for agreement of the present participle, and if this were so, forms such as stante, regnante might rather be considered as syntactical phenomena, which would argue against including them in a count of third declension plural forms without -s.

Three main theories have been advanced to account for the establishment of the -i plural in third declension nouns: (1) analogy with the second declension,[9] (2) closing influence of final -s,[10] and (3) possibility of double development of front vowels in the final syllable.[11] With regard to the possibility of analogy with the second declension, the distinct gradation of the occurrence of the forms without -s argues strongly against it, since if it were simply a matter of borrowing a plural from another declension, one would expect to find less strict correspondence with the phonetic fall of final -s. The figures also argue against the theory of the closing influence of the final -s, since if this were so, the table ought to show that wherever the -i form occurs there should also be a predominance of the use of -is as opposed to -es.

The double development theory seems, however, to fit in more exactly with the evidence of the documents. Geographically, the frequency of appearance of the form without -s corresponds exactly to the phonological fall of -s (Cf. Paragraph 3.3). The documents show also that there was a confusion of the front vowel phonemes in unaccented position (Cf. Paragraph 2.8). Since using the traditional -es plural without the -s would have created identity with the singular, it seems most logical to suppose that, since the alternate possibility existed, the -i ending would take over the plural connotation. It is not here disputed that the fact that -i was the regular plural of the second declension must have made easier the generalization of the -i plural in the third declension.[12]

It is noteworthy that in Central Italy there occur two place names also with the -i plural ending: ad Ruchi (ruges) in document No. 191, and ad Colli (colles) in document No. 179, both from Lucca.

10. Neuter Plurals

10.1 Neuter Plurals of the second declension

Nominative	-a	-as	-is	-am	-ae	-es
Siena	3	-	3	-	-	-
Pisa	5	-	-	-	-	-
Lucca	67	2	6	2	3	-
Piacenza	-	-	-	-	-	-
North. It.	-	-	-	-	1	1

Examples: qui sunt ... sistariorum duas (113); id est terra, vinea, pratis ... olivitis ... (42); ipse edificia (113); dona nostra ... permaneat confermatam (16); anteposito tectora quae ... positae sunt et quinquagenta iuges terra quas Adoald ... emere debit (137).

Genitive	-orum	-a	-is
Siena	-	1	-
Pisa	3	3	-
Lucca	15	1	2
Piacenza	-	-	-
North. It.	3	-	-

Examples: de pondera peccata mea deprecare (171); pondere peccata relaxare (171); meis dotalium pagina (145); quam beneficiis chartul(am) (35).

Dative does not occur.

Accusative	-a	-as	-am	-is	-ae	-es
Siena	19	1	-	2	-	-
Pisa	13	-	-	-	-	-
Lucca	115	17	1	11	22	-
Piacenza	15	6	-	1	-	-
North. It.	14	4	-	-	-	2

Examples: ipsas duas iugis ... dono (291); qui alias suprascriptas capitulas facias (138); fini (adv.) signa posite (161); ad ipse sancte loca (194); quinquagenta iuges emere debit (137).

Ablative	-is	-a	-as	-i	-ae	-es	-os	-am
Siena	2	1	1	-	-	-	-	-
Pisa	11	3	-	1	-	-	-	-
Lucca	188	54	12	7	3	1	1	1
Piacenza	13	14	1	2	-	-	-	-
North. It.	10	3	2	-	-	-	-	-

Examples: cum omnis edificia suas (148); in alie loca (115); cum edificia constructe (115); in isti futuri seculi (136); in perpetui temporibus (46); cum omnis aliis edificiis et fundamenti (255); cum fundamenta sua (113); pro meis delicta (171).

The important points to note in connection with the second declension neuter plural are the extension of the -a ending to the genitive and ablative, and the addition of -s. The table below gives the total number of occurrences of -a and -as, and the percentage of addition of -s.

	-a	-as	%
Siena	24	2	8%
Pisa	24	-	-
Lucca	237	31	12%
Piacenza	29	7	19%
North. It.	17	6	26%

The -as ending appears in all cases of the noun, to a somewhat greater extent, however, in the two northern groups of documents with apparent gradation from north to south. This seems to indicate that the appearance of the -as ending does not represent merely incorrect addition of -s, but that there was actual confusion with the feminine plurals, since the as plural in the first declension is definitely more frequent in the north.[13]

10.2 Neuter Plural of the third declension

Neuter plurals of the third declension do not occur very frequently in the nominative, genitive and dative cases. In the nominative, there are 49 instances of the normal -a ending in Lucca plus one nominative plural in -es (omnia nobis pertinentes - 235), and the sole other third declension neuter nominative plural is a form in -ibus occurring in a document from Siena (nostris meruerint operibus - 248). The normal genitive plural in -ium occurs 23 times in the Lucca documents, plus two instances of -ia also in Lucca (omnia in integrum mediaetate - 165, omnia mediaetatem - 144). The dative does not occur at all.

The table which follows gives complete figures for all occurrences of the accusative and ablative.

Accusative	-a	-ibus	-is	-e	-es	-as
Siena	10	-	-	-	-	2
Pisa	17	2	-	-	-	-
Lucca	138	12	3	1	1	5
Piacenza	9	-	-	-	-	2
North. It.	15	-	-	-	-	1

Examples: offero . . . omnem substantia nostra . . . mobilia vel inmobilia seo se moventibus (194); omnia ad nos pertenentes offerre (194).

Ablative	-ibus	-a	-as	-es	-is	-i	-e(m)
Siena	12	5	1	1	1	-	-
Pisa	23	11	1	1	4	1	1
Lucca	143	83	2	1	10	-	1
Piacenza	5	11	1	-	-	-	-
North. It.	11	12	-	-	1	-	-

Examples: ex iura parentum (73); cum omnia adiacentia sua (73); cum omnias que supra positas habes (66); de omnia nutrimina mea (235); cum nutriminas magioris et menuris (193); pro facinora nostra (165); cunctis perhennis temporibus (165).

There is little comment which can be made about the neuter plural of the third declension. In the ablative, the -a ending occurs to a similar degree as in the second declension neuter plural. The -as ending also appears, but occurrences are too sporadic to indicate any geographical distribution.

CONCLUSION

Before beginning the discussion of the conclusions which may be drawn from the evidence of the texts, it seems advisable to present a table summarizing what may be considered the "key phenomena" in the question of the state of dialectization in the Eighth Century. The phenomena on the table below have been numbered to facilitate reference to them, however otherwise the table is self-explanatory.

		Siena	Pisa	Lucca	Piacenza	North. It.
*1.	Change of final $\breve{e}$, $\bar{i}$, $\breve{o}$	0.6	1.4	1.5	6.8	4.1
*2.	Voicing of interv. occlusives	-	-	0.1	-	10.4
*3.	Fall of final -t	9.5	3.4	5.0	2.0	4.2
*4.	Fall of final -s	3.3	2.1	1.6	0.9	0.4
5.	I Decl. Plural as>a	26%	20%	18%	3%	5%
6.	II Decl. Plural is>i	43%	35%	36%	41%	9%
7.	III Decl. Plural is,es>i,e	12%	19%	12%	5%	5%
8.	Nom. Sing. II Decl. o, u, um for us	36%	29%	28%	18%	15%
9.	Gen. Sing. III Decl. i, e for is	34%	26%	28%	18%	23%
10.	Acc. Pl. II Decl. is, i for os, us	54%	61%	44%	65%	20%
11.	Acc. Pl. I Decl. ae for as, a	12%	7%	6%	-	2%

* The figures given for these phenomena represent the occurrence per 100 lines of text.

Making reference in each instance to the various phenomena as numbered on the table, the following interesting facts must be pointed out with regard to the theory of the Spezia-Rimini line as an early dialectal divide:

1. Phenomena 1, 5, and 7 can be considered as evidence in favor of the existence of the Spezia-Rimini line in the Eighth Century.

2. Phenomena 2, 6 and 10 indicate that in the Eighth Century the river Po might have been a dialectal border.

3. All other phenomena (3, 4, 8, 9, 11) occur in fairly regular gradation from south to north, arguing against the existence of any distinct dialectal divide.

4. Even phenomena 1 and 5, which occur with significant difference in frequency in the areas to the north and south of the so-called Spezia-Rimini line, show a distinct south to north gradation in the three Central Italian groups of documents. Such evidence would in any event argue strongly against the contention that the Spezia-Rimini line was an early divide, existing from the end of the Second Century as Von Wartburg has maintained.[1] For if this had been the case, one would certainly be justified in expecting to find the phenomena occurring at approximately the same rate in the various localities on the southern side of the dividing line, and not in regularly gradated frequencies.

Certainly the fact that the fall of final -s appears with regularly diminishing frequency from south to north, while the voicing of intervocalic occlusives occurs only North of the Po and not in Piacenza, which is also well north of the Spezia-Rimini line, presents a strong argument against the theory that there existed an early dialectal divide, to the north of which intervocalic occlusives were voiced and -s retained, while to the south intervocalic occlusives remained unvoiced while -s fell.

Aside from those phenomena which are particularly pertinent in connection with the Spezia-Rimini line theory, the documents show that there existed in the Eighth Century other phenomena which are certainly valid dialectal differences. Among these are the following:

1. The tendency to use the more closed pronunciation of vowels in Central Italy, as shown by the greater frequency of the -i orthography for front vowels, and the -u orthography for back vowels, in the documents from Siena, Pisa and Lucca.

2. In the proper names of the second declension, the greater prevalence of the use of no inflectional ending in Northern Italy, and the tendency in Central Italy to generalize the -i ending in all cases.

3. The occurrence of the -u ending for -us or -um, confined almost exclusively to the Central Italian documents.

4. The possibility of the diphthongization of accented ō in free position, as indicated by the relatively high frequency of the ō u change in this position, which is contrary to the general tendencies of vowel development in the North Italian documents. (Cf. Paragraph 1.3).

A correlation should be pointed out between two of the phenomena listed on the summary table, regarding the plural of the first declension: lines 5 and 11 indicate that in the north the retention of final -s in the plural was quite literally necessitated by the fact that the -ae plural was virtually unknown--note that on line 11 the 2% figure for Northern Italy is accounted for by one single occurrence of -ae in the plural.

From the table it will be further observed that in general, fall of -s in the plural is considerably higher wherever such fall does not cause morphological confusion with the singular; for example, is>i in the second declension is much more frequent than as>a in the first declension or is, es>i in the third. However, in the genitive singular of the third declension, fall of -s is noticeably higher throughout, since here the plural form generalized in the documents retains -s, and there is therefore no morphological resistance to fall of -s in the singular.

Corroboration of certain trends of development indicated by this study seems furnished by comparison with evidence from the later documents (after 774) of the study by R. Politzer and the French documents studied by M. A. Pei.[2] Unfortunately the comparison can be made for only a few phenomena, as the different methods of counting and tabulating used in the three studies do not always furnish the correct basis for comparing frequencies: for example, Pei does not furnish information concerning number of lines of text, nor does he count retention of -us, while Politzer figures everything, including vowel changes, on a percentage basis. Nevertheless, a few interesting points can be brought out. On lines 5 and 6 of the table on page 33 note that the relative frequency of the fall of final -s in the first and second declension plural definitely shows that the impulse for this change came from the south, traveling northward; R. Politzer's documents show that in the region north of the Po, between 774 and 799, the rate of this change was 22% in the first declension and 29% in the second,[3] showing that later in the century the impulse to drop -s became stronger also in the north. This change does not occur at all in the French documents studied by Pei.[4]

Further indication of the increased fall of -s later in the century is furnished by the substitution of -o, -u, -um for -us in the second declension, which occurs with a frequency of 30% of all instances after 774[5] (Cf. lines 8 and 9 of the table on page 33).

In the accusative plural of the second declension, the substitution of -i, -is for -os, -us--line 10 on the summary table--is 38% after 774,[6] indicating that the substitution of a distinctive vowel to preserve the plural connotation was necessitated by the increased fall of -s, which was causing identity with the singular. The occurrence of this substitution in the French documents is 18%.[7]

To summarize the conclusions indicated by the evidence presented in this study, the picture revealed by the documents is that there must have been somewhere south of Toscanella--perhaps even in the Toscanella area itself--a center where the fall of final consonants, and particularly of final -s, began and from which the phenomenon was spreading during the Eighth Century. There is some evidence of the existence of a dialectal divide as regards the voicing of intervocalic occlusives, however this line which may have existed in the Eighth Century certainly does not coincide with the present line of dialectization between Northern and Central Italian.

The documents certainly show that there was indeed dialectization in the Eighth Century. They do not--they can not--show just when the dialectization began in the center of innovation.

Evidence presented in the studies by Proskauer and Cross shows that up to the Sixth Century certain phenomena--namely the fall of -s and syncopation--occurred sporadically throughout the Romance world, and thus seems to cast doubt on the existence of dialectization at that time.[8] However the validity of the evidence of these studies on a statistical basis can be questioned, since the phenomena are not evaluated in terms of their relative frequency, and since indeed the possibility of statistical evaluation of inscriptional material poses a great problem, first because of the extremely stereotyped nature of the inscriptions, and second because of the very sporadic occurrences of variations in a tremendous mass of material.

It seems unwarranted to assume that cultural and social developments in the Eighth Century led to the creation of the Romance languages,[9] since it is obvious from the linguistic developments shown in the documents that in the Eighth Century there existed all the features which later became the basic differences between the Romance tongues. Among the most important of these are the voicing of intervocalic occlusives--practically non-existent in Central Italy, frequent in Italy north of the Po, and also in France[10]--and treatment of final vowels and final -s--in Central Italy the final vowels remain distinct and -s falls to a considerable degree, in France -s remains almost completely stable,[11] while final vowels including i become indistinct.[12]

Thus the state of the final syllable in the Eighth Century foretells the choice of the vowel as the morphologically significant feature in Central Italy. In Northern Italy, the greater retention of -s, combined with the apparently greater instability of the final vowel, seems to indicate that temporarily at least the -s plural was the preferred morphological feature; however the sharp increase of fall of -s after 774 shows that still in the Eighth Century, Northern Italy began to conform to developments in Central Italy. In France the final -s was almost completely stable at the beginning of the Eighth Century, while the final vowel had become quite indistinct.

It thus seems entirely reasonable to assume that the causes of the divergence of the Romance languages antedated the Eighth Century, and a careful examination on a quantitative comparative basis of all existing documentary and inscriptional material can be expected to shed further light on this essential problem of Romance Philology.

Part II

ON THE ORIGIN OF FRENCH ROMANCE

INTRODUCTION

1. Purpose

In Part I of our study it was shown how two important trends were at work in the formative period of Romance: the trend to drop final consonants was during the Eighth Century travelling northward from Central to Northern Italy; the other opposing trend to reduce vowel phonemes in the final syllable was associated with a greater stress accent and was travelling geographically in the opposite direction, namely from north to south.

The question which poses itself is of course the time of origin of those two trends within the Romance world. The question of the time of origin of the tendency to drop final consonants cannot be answered by the method employed in our study--namely the analysis of Late Latin texts--since no Vulgar Latin documentary material from Central Italy is available for the period preceding the Eighth Century. However the question of the time of the intensification of the stress accent can be investigated with the help of Late Latin documents. It is to this investigation that Part II of this work will be devoted.

The Romance dialect in the formative period of which the intensification of the stress accent played the most important role was evidently Northern French. It is in the Northern French speech group that fall of vowels in the final syllable, syncopation of unaccented vowels, voicing and effacement of intervocalic occlusives are carried farther than in any other large Romance group. Thus it seems only logical to assume that most probably an early center of the intensification of the stress accent lay in Northern France.

It is particularly fortunate that there are original documents from the Northern French area available which enable us to push our investigation back to the early Seventh Century. The second part of this study is therefore an analysis of Seventh and early Eighth Century documents, undertaken by the same method that was utilized in Part I. But while Part I of this study attempts to show differences from area to area, Part II is concerned with differences in time.

The phonological phenomena selected for investigation are with a few exceptions the same as were studied in the Italian documents, the chief exception being the fall of final consonants which for all practical purposes does not occur in the French texts. No count of morphological phenomena was included in the second part, primarily because such a study has already been undertaken[1] and also because this study intentionally limits itself to the investigation of the trend toward an intensified stress accent.

2. Description of Material

The material chosen for the purpose of this investigation consists of the original documents found in the Tardif collection.[2] The time limits set for the period to be investigated were 625 to 717. The limit of 625 corresponds to the earliest available document. The limit of 717 is imposed by the fact that no original documents written between 717 and 750 are available, and that the original documents written after 750 seem under the influence of deliberate attempts to restore classical Latin orthography.[3] The frequency of orthographic substitution found in these texts is thus determined by a factor not present in the earlier texts. This, of course, makes the post-750 texts unsuitable for the type of comparative study which was undertaken.

The documents investigated are primarily royal charters and diplomas of the Merovingian kings. Only a few (Tardif Nos. 19, 24, 26, 29, 36, 39) are private legal documents (e.g. donations, testaments). In their general context and vocabulary the documents are extremely similar to the Italian documents investigated in Part I of this study. Those documents of the Tardif collection which are royal charters are also available in the edition of Ph. Lauer and Ph. Samaran.[4] The latter edition which is somewhat more modern and accurate than that of Tardif and which also includes photostatic reproductions of original documents was available as a check on the Tardif edition and used as such in certain important instances. One of the documents studied (L. and S. No. 28) is not included in the Tardif collection and is available in the Lauer and Samaran edition exclusively. Two documents were excluded from the investigation even though they were originals, because they cannot be dated with reasonable certainty: Tardif No. 40 which is dated approximately 700 by Tardif but which should probably be dated in the Seventh Century[5] and Tardif No. 27, which Tardif dates 650 to 750 and Lauer and Samaran 629 to 639.

For the purpose of the investigation the documents were divided in four groups according to time periods. The time periods chosen were determined by the dating of the documents, which in some cases is possible only within certain ten or twenty year periods. The documents of Group IV had previously been thoroughly investigated by M. A. Pei in his study of the Eighth Century texts in Northern France. The statistics presented in his work were in some cases utilized as a check on the accuracy of our findings.

A summary table of the documents used in this study follows:

		No. of Documents	No. of Scribes	No. of Lines*
Period I	625-640	5	5	135
Period II	653-680	11	11	508
Period III	681-699	17	15	1066
Period IV	700-717	10	8	564

* In counting the number of lines, some adjustment was made for half lines or lines in which several words were missing or illegible.

From the table it will be noted that the first part of the Seventh Century is underrepresented as far as number of lines is concerned. This will unfortunately have some effect on the significance of the findings of this study. But again it is hoped that the comparative approach and the care not to base too much significance on one single phenomenon will minimize the error which may result from the inequality of the samples available for the four periods.

SELECTED PHONOLOGICAL PHENOMENA

1. Accented Vowels

1.0 In accented position practically the only orthographic substitutions occurring in the texts are the confusions of $\breve{\imath}$ and $\bar{e}$ and $\breve{u}$ and $\bar{o}$ to represent the /ẹ/ and /ọ/ phonemes.

1.1 The tabulation for the confusion of i and e follows:

$\bar{e} > \breve{\imath}$	Free	Checked	Monosyl.	Total	Occ. per 100 lines
I	4 (2.9)	3 (2.2)	-	7	5.1
II	82 (20.4)	10 (1.9)	-	92	22.3
III	179 (18.1)	38 (3.5)	2	219	21.8
IV	124 (23.1)	26 (4.4)	-	140	27.5

Examples: mercide (11); consinsi ($\bar{e}$ before ns was counted as $\bar{e}$ in free position); rigni (11); tris (30).

$\breve{\imath} > e$	Free	Checked	Monosyl.	Total	Occ. per 100 lines
I	7	-	-	7	5.2
II	8	-	-	8	1.5
III	21	-	-	21	1.9
IV	15	-	-	15	2.7

Examples: ligetimo (17).

The most pronounced change in the frequency of occurrence of the above substitution of e for ĭ and i for ē seems to be the increase of the i for /ẹ/ orthography in Period II. This possible explanation can be suggested: Since the increase of i for ē is accompanied by a fairly pronounced decrease of e for ĭ (5.2 to 1.5), the pronunciation of the e sound may have become closer during the second period, thus suggesting the i orthography rather than the e orthography for the rendition of the /ẹ/ phoneme. Another possible explanation is suggested by the fact that the marked increase in the i for /ẹ/ orthography seems to occur in free position only. The increase in the i orthography can therefore be connected with the French diphthongization of free /ē/. In the latter case the i orthography may be an attempt to represent the diphthongized /ẹ/ sound (Cf. savir and podir in the Oaths of Strasbourg).

1.2 In the back vowel phonemes we find again the representation of the /ọ/ phoneme by u and o. The distribution of the substitution of u for Classical Latin ō and o for Classical Latin ŭ is as follows:

ŭ>o	Free	Checked	Monosyl.	Total
I	-	-	-	-
II	-	-	-	-
III	2	4	-	6
IV	1	1	-	2

Examples: estodiant (35), poplicus (37).

ō>u	Free	Checked	Monosyl.	Total	Occ. per 100 lines
I	2	3	-	5	3.7
II	11	8	2	21	4.1
III	13	21	11	45	4.2
IV	8	13	5	26	4.6

Examples: geneturi (6); nuscetur (5), nus (20); urdene (38).

The change of ŭ>o is so extremely scarce that one can hardly draw any conclusion as to differences between the four periods. The very fact of the rarity of the change, however, may be indicative of the extremely close pronunciation of the /ọ/ phoneme, suggesting to the scribe the u rather than the o orthography. The substitution of u for Classical Latin ō is, on the other hand, very frequent, and shows a slight but definite trend toward increase from one period to the other. This seems to indicate that the /ọ/ phoneme became progressively closer in pronunciation and tended to shift its point of articulation toward the /u/ phoneme. It is of particular interest that this process apparently took place during the Seventh and Eighth Centuries, for the shifting of the /u/ phoneme forward to the ü pronunciation can be explained precisely as a response of the linguistic system which wanted to avoid the falling together of the /ọ/ and /u/ phonemes.[1]

2. Unaccented Vowels

2.0 The method of counting the unaccented vowels has been the same as that employed in studying the Italian documents. Here again (Cf. Part I, 2.0) the instances of confusion in the final syllable, where morphological considerations may outweigh the phonological factors, have not been included.

2.1 The confusion of the e and i orthography for the presentation of the /ẹ/ phoneme in unaccented position occurs with considerable frequency. The statistics for the e orthography for Classical Latin ĭ and the i orthography for Classical Latin ē follow. The rate of occurrence per hundred lines is given in parentheses after each figure.

	Initial		Pretonic Uninitial		Atonic Penult
	ē>i	ĭ>e	ē>i	ĭ>e	ĭ>e
I	3 (2.2)	3 (2.2)	1 (0.7)	17 (12.6)	55 (40.7)
II	8 (1.6)	12 (2.4)	5 (0.9)	62 (12.2)	163 (32.1)
III	26 (2.4)	25 (2.3)	7 (0.6)	109 (10.2)	164 (15.4)
IV	23 (4.1)	24 (4.2)	5 (0.9)	108 (19.1)	160 (28.4)

Examples: ĕ>i: ficisse (13); vindederat (14); aeclisiarum (19).
ĭ>e: auturetate, pontefecebus (11); stabele (4); termenandum (14).

The figures do not seem to reveal any particular trend. The most striking figure is the relatively low number of occurrences of e for ĭ in the atonic penult during the third period. It is caused by several scribes who seem to adhere somewhat more to the correct orthography than most of their colleagues. The documents in which the substitution of e for ĭ in the atonic penult is particularly rare are 37 and 39. Both are private documents and the scribes of those documents may have been trained in a somewhat different tradition of orthography than the royal scribes who are the writers of the majority of our documents. At any rate, the scribes displaying the tendency toward a classically correct spelling of ĭ in the atonic penult do not seem to show the same tendency with regard to any other phenomenon: thus the scribe of document 39, who in his 37 lines of text is responsible for only one e spelling for Latin unaccented ĭ (nomene), substitutes o for unaccented ŭ 7 times (epistola, stipolacione), i for unaccented ĕ 12 times (debiat, habit).

2.2 In the presentation of the statistics of the u and o orthography for the /o̜/ phoneme the orthographic substitutions in final syllable have again been excluded, since in most instances they should be considered from the morphological rather than the phonetic point of view.

	Initial		Pretonic Uninitial		Atonic Penult
	ō>u	ŭ>o	ō>u	ŭ>o	ŭ>o
I	2	2	2	2	7 (5.2)
II	1	7	4	11	9 (1.7)
III	1	14	7	21	33 (3.1)
IV	10	12	6	8	26 (4.6)

Examples: ō>u: nuscuntur (6), neguciante (4).
ŭ>o: jobemus, postolatur (11), singola (4).

The substitution of u for ō is infrequent and the distribution of the more frequent o for ŭ seems too erratic to justify the drawing of any conclusions.

2.3 The behavior of short ĕ (>/e̜/) in unaccented position is of particular interest from the point of view of our investigation, since--as was shown in Part I (2.4 and Conclusion)--the weakening of open e to closed e in unaccented position can be interpreted as a direct result of stress accent conditions. The instances of substitution of the i orthography for Classical Latin ĕ, indicating fusion of /e̜/ and /e̩/, are tabulated as follows:

ĕ>i	Initial	Pret. Unin.	At. Pen.	Final	Hiatus	Total	Occ. per 100 lines
I	-	-	-	5	-	5	3.7
II	1	1	4	39	33	78	15.3
III	-	2	26	152	46	226	21.2
IV	7	2	4	83	38	134	23.7

Examples: tilenariis (47), inpidimento (50), facire (19), oportit (11), liciat (11).

The above table shows that the substitution of i for /ẹ/ (<ĕ) in unaccented position follows a definite and unmistakable trend. This substitution increases sharply in the second period and continues that trend toward increase throughout the following periods. The conclusion suggested is that a definite increase in stress accent took place sometime in the middle of the Seventh Century and that the stress accent continued to become increasingly stronger throughout the period under investigation.

2.4 The substitution of u for /ọ/(<ŏ) in unaccented position indicates the weakening of /ọ/ to /ǫ/ and should thus, like the substitution of i for ĕ in the same position, be interpreted as an indication of stress accent conditions. The statistics for the u orthography for Classical Latin unaccented ŏ follow:

ŏ>u	Initial	Pret. Unin.	At. Pen.	Final	Total	Occ. per 100 lines
I	-	1	-	-	1	0.7
II	1	-	1	1	3	0.6
III	6	2	4	18	30	2.9
IV	1	-	8	5	14	2.5

Examples: bunuaria (39), Diunensi (7), corpure (34), creatur (34).

The orthography of u for Classical Latin o does not occur with impressive frequency. It is extremely sporadic during the first two periods, but increases quite definitely in Periods III and IV. Thus u for ŏ in unaccented position seems to follow the trend of i for ĕ in the same position. This parallel is of course the behavior one should expect, since a weakening of ẹ to ę should normally be accompanied by the parallel weakening of ọ to ǫ. At any rate, the orthographic substitutions of u for ŏ corroborate the conclusion presented in the preceding paragraph: a definite increase in the intensity of the stress accent appears to have taken place at the middle of the Seventh Century.

2.5 Of the extreme vowels /i/ and /u/, only /i/ reveals any important changes in orthographic presentation. In either case one could expect a significant orthographic confusion only in the final syllable or intertonic syllables in which the two vowels were destined to fall in Old French. The substitution of o for ū in final syllable, however, is a purely morphological phenomenon (absorption of the 4th declension by the 2nd). Thus only the behavior of long ī in unaccented position was investigated and is statistically presented in the following table:

ī>e	Initial	Pret. Unin.	Final	Total	Occ. per 100 lines
I	-	-	-	-	-
II	3	2	18 (3.5)	23	4.5
III	-	-	53 (4.9)	53	4.9
IV	3	3	65 (11.5)	71	12.5

Examples: delacione (44), requeratur (47), fisce nostri (genitive, 31), vise sunt (masc. plural, 30).

The distribution of the substitution of e for unaccented ī of Classical Latin shows the following important facts: The e orthography is sporadic in all but the final syllable. It is completely absent during the first period. It appears only in the second period and then shows a definite trend toward increase. In other words the general distribution of the phenomenon follows that noted previously for weakening of unaccented ọ and ẹ. From the phonemic point of view the substitution of e for ī in final syllable in our texts can be explained in two different ways: It may be an effort to reestablish the symmetry of the vowel system in the final syllable from o a e i to o a e, for the final syllable knew only one back vowel /o/ after the fourth declension had become absorbed by the second. Or the substitution of e for ī may reflect the trend to reduce all phonemes in the final syllable to one indefinite vowel. In the light of subsequent developments in Old French and of the correlation of the e substitution for ī, with the weakening of unaccented /ẹ/ and /ọ/ and thus with the intensification of the stress accent, the second explanation seems more likely.

The substitution of e for ī occurs primarily in the plural of the second declension, but it is of interest to note that the appearance of the active for the passive infinitive in the second, third, and fourth conjugations correlates perfectly with the e for ī substitution in the declensional system: this seems to prove that this confusion of active and passive infinitive is a purely phonetic phenomenon.[2] For instance the scribes of the first period write the usual formula closing the documents: eam decrevimus roborari (Tardif 5, 6). The first scribe (Tardif 11) to confuse i with e in the plural of the second declension (vise fuimus) writes also decrivemus roborare.[3]

3. Consonantal Phenomena

3.0 The consonantal phenomena included in this study are the voicing and so-called unvoicing of intervocalic occlusives and the simplification and gemination of intervocalic consonants. These phenomena may be structurally connected, since the voicing of the intervocalic occlusives in France can be considered as part of a structural change that replaces a chain of opposition of double:single unvoiced:voiced by a chain of single:voiced:fricative.[4]

3.1 The distribution of instances of voicing and unvoicing of intervocalic occlusives during the four periods is as follows:

	Voicing	Occ. per 100 lines	Unvoicing	Occ. per 100 lines
I	-	0	-	0
II	8	1.6	6	1.1
III	11	1.1	4	0.4
IV	28	4.9	-	0

Examples: voicing - segundo (22), estibulacione (24), podibat (13), plagabile (46), audentico (26).
unvoicing - opidiencia (21), congrecatio (34).

From this distribution it will be noted that voicing sets in with the second period and remains on about the same level of frequency during the third period and increases considerably during the fourth period. It is also of interest to note that the general uncertainty as to the pronunciation of the intervocalic plosive which is attested by the unvoicing during the second and third periods ceases with period IV. The pattern of the voicing follows those of the other phenomena which can be connected with the increased intensity of the stress accent.

3.2 The distribution of simplification and gemination is given in the following table:

	Simplification	Occ. per 100 lines	Gemination	Occ. per 100 lines
I	-	0	-	0
II	1	0.2	8	1.6
III	1	0.1	21	1.9
IV	30	5.3	17	3.1

Examples: simplification - terena (19), opidum (42), vilas (41).
gemination - jobimmus (38), tuttum (43).

The simplification and gemination pattern reveals that apparently with the beginning of period II the phonemic differentiation between long and short (double and single) consonants had become doubtful to the scribes, who thus confound single and double consonants orthographically. It is of particular interest to note that except for isolated instances simplification does not set in until the beginning of the Eighth Century. The implication is that during the second half of the Seventh Century the general phonemic pattern of differentiation of intervocalic consonants must have been double:single voiced:fricative after Latin tt:t:d had changed to tt:d:ð. During the period in which t:d had already changed to d:ð but the double consonants had not yet simplified to take the place of the single unvoiced, a voiced and unvoiced plosive were not opposed to each other in intervocalic position. This may account for the existence of the reverse phenomenon of unvoicing during periods II and III, and the sudden disappearance of the reverse phenomenon in period IV as soon as simplification sets in in impressive numbers.

4. Summary

In the following table we summarize in terms of the frequency per 100 lines of text the essential phenomena studied in Part II of this investigation. The orthographic substitutions which can be directly associated with intensified stress accent are listed first. The i̱ orthography for /ẹ/ in free position, which (as mentioned in paragraph 1.1) may indicate diphthongization of /ẹ/ and thus be associated with stress accent conditions, is tabulated apart from the "stress accent phenomena", but not included among those which can definitely not be associated with increased intensity of stress accent.

	"Stress accent phenomena"					ẹ̄[>i̱	"Non-stress accent phenomena"					
	ĕ>i̱	ŏ>u̱	-ī>e̱	V.	Simp.		ē̱[>i̱	i̱>e̱	ō̱>u̱	ē̱>i̱	ĭ>e̱	ŭ>o̱
I	3.7	0.7	-	-	-	2.9	2.2	5.2	3.7	2.9	55.5	8.1
II	15.3	0.6	4.5	1.6	0.2	20.4	1.9	1.5	4.1	2.5	46.7	5.3
III	21.2	2.9	4.9	1.1	0.1	18.1	3.5	1.9	4.2	3.0	29.9	6.4
IV	23.7	2.5	12.5	4.9	5.3	23.1	4.4	2.7	4.6	5.0	51.7	8.1

The general frequency of stress accent phenomena during the four periods may thus be summarized as follows, by combining within each period the frequency of all five phenomena mentioned: Period I: 4.4, Period II: 22.2, Period III: 30.2, Period IV: 48.9. A comparable summary of the frequency per 100 lines of the orthographic substitutions which cannot be directly connected with the intensified stress accent reads as follows: Period I: 82.0, Period II: 62.0, Period III: 48.9, Period IV: 76.5.

One conclusion becomes obvious from the comparison of the relative frequency of stress accent connected and non-stress accent connected orthographic substitution: the steady increase in the frequency of the substitutions which testify to an intensified stress accent can under no circumstances be accounted for by increasing scribal ignorance. It must correspond to an actual strong increase in the intensity of the stress accent which made itself felt in Northern French speech from the middle of the Seventh Century on. And it was this increase in stress accent with its resulting fall of final vowels, syncopation of the atonic penult, voicing and effacement of intervocalic surds, which gave to French Romance its most characteristic features.

Our findings, it should be pointed out, are quite consistent with the opinions held by many eminent authorities. Meyer-Lübke suggested that the characteristic features of French were developed in the 6th and 7th centuries and connects their appearance with the immigration of the Franks.[5] A similar view is held by Walter von Wartburg,[6] and Elise Richter in her important chronology of French suggested that practically all specifically "French" features of French speech were created sometime between the 5th and 8th centuries by an intensified stress accent which she in turn links to the appearance of the Germanic superstratum.[7] A brief comparison of our findings with those of Elise Richter is of particular interest. In her work she puts the simplification of geminates in the 8th century (par. 171), and the extreme weakening of most unaccented vowels into an indefinite vowel sound (reflected in our documents by the increasing inability of the scribes to distinguish unaccented open and closed e, and especially final i and e) in the 6th-7th centuries (par. 157). The diphthongization of ẹ (and ọ) is assumed to have taken place in the 5th-6th centuries (par. 146)--and--except for an isolated development icus>igus (3rd-5th century, par. 82), the voicing of intervocalic stops is considered a 4th-6th century development (par. 121, 118, 123). Again these findings, we feel, are quite consistent with ours, if we keep in mind that E. Richter attempts to establish the chronology of a popular speech which she feels is quite isolated from the social stratum of the more educated (p. 16). Her chronology is thus based on first occurrences and she is not concerned with the element of increasing statistical frequencies. That some of her chronologies antedate the ones we suggest is thus not surprising. She is concerned with the initial appearance of a phenomenon, while we were tracing its increasing expansion into a different social stratum.

Of all the phenomena that we have studied, the voicing of intervocalic stops seems to have the most controversial chronology. Our findings seem to suggest the 7th century, Elise Richter puts most of the Northern French voicings into the 4th-6th centuries, Walter von Wartburg feels that in most of the Western Romance world voicing was accomplished by the beginning of the 3rd century.[8] His evidence is based on fairly isolated inscriptional examples, which are rejected as sufficient evidence by Elise Richter.[9] These chronologies may of course not be mutually incompatible. Voicing may have started at certain isolated points and it may have taken several centuries for the phenomenon to gain its ultimate geographical and social expansion. Menendez Pidal furnished considerable evidence that in Spain, for instance, at a very late date, voicing was complete in Leonese, still resisted by the Latin of the upper strata of Castilian and absent in Aragonese[10] where, as it is well known, there are still today areas never reached by the voicing process.[11] Whether the early instances of voicing upon which von Wartburg's chronology is based have any connection with the later process of voicing in the chronology of Elise Richter is of crucial importance for our interpretation. If they have, then the voicing of intervocalic stops could not possibly be connected with the intensification of the stress accent caused by a Germanic superstratum. The correlation of simplification and voicing with the "stress accent phenomena" would then be accidental--a possibility which exists linguistically as well as statistically and which must be admitted (cf. footnote 4 above). On the other hand, the early instances of voicing could be indicative only of a more or less sporadic lenition of unvoiced stops such as for instance exists in the Roman or Umbrian area.[12] In this study we suggest the latter possibility and assume on the basis of the statistical evidence a connection of voicing to stress accent intensification. Yet the above-mentioned possibility of an accidental rather than a causal connection between the two must also be admitted and further investigated.

Part III

SYNTHESIS OF PREVIOUS FINDINGS BY STUDY OF SCRIBAL HABITS

1. Purpose and Method

The purpose of Part III of this study is to re-investigate the material presented in Parts I and II by using a different method of examination. This new approach serves not only as a check on the accuracy of the results obtained so far, but will enable us also to draw a comparison between the findings of the analyses of the Eighth Century French and Italian texts.

The presentation of the statistics in the first two parts of this study, those of Part I derived from groups of documents arranged according to geographic locations, those of Part II derived from groups of documents arranged according to chronological period, could obviously not take into account existing variations among the orthographic habits of individual scribes within the groups. Each individual has-- to a certain extent, at least--his own orthographic peculiarities, and had perhaps--again within limits --his own phonemic speech pattern. Obviously a single scribe who displays to the extreme a liking for one particular orthographic variation can decisively influence the entire statistics for his period or region. This danger is the more to be considered, because actually the number of lines contributed by individual scribes varies considerably. Any scribe contributing a large proportion of lines of text to a particular group of documents may of course unduly influence the statistics presented, which are thus in danger of being not as truly representative of the period or area under consideration as one could wish. In addition, one should also keep in mind that the orthographic variations of the individual scribes are interpreted from a phonemic point of view, and considered as indications of features of the phonemic structure of the speech of the writer. From this point of view, the frequency with which an individual scribe uses a certain orthographic variant is of course not necessarily significant. The important conclusion may be drawn not from the frequency of an orthographic variant, but from its absence or presence as the case may be.

In the third part of this study the material within each period or area was not treated as an homogeneous group, but the documents were arranged within each group according to their writers. Documents originally written by one writer but later recopied by another were not considered. The signatures and testimonial formulas ending the various documents were not taken into consideration if they were not written by the scribe responsible for the main body of the document. An effort was made then to determine essential elements of the phonological pattern of each individual scribe using either presence or absence of an orthographic variation as the only criterion. Thus if a scribe substituted i for $\breve{e}$ in unaccented position only once he was considered as showing a phonemic pattern without differentiation of $ę$ and $ẹ$ in unaccented position, just as the scribe who made the same substitution ten or fifteen times. This point of view introduces of course the possible danger of attributing significance to the accidental, but the danger of this type of error lies in the opposite direction from the danger of attributing too much significance to the scribe who shows the variation very frequently, which was present in Parts I and II. This very fact makes the method of Part III an effective check on the accuracy of the previous findings.

To minimize a further possible source of inaccuracy, only such phonological or morphological phenomena were included as occur frequently enough in all documents to give almost every scribe a fair chance to display a given phonological or morphological variation. Nevertheless it is of course inevitable that a scribe contributing 500 lines of text has a greater opportunity to commit at least one orthographic substitution of a given type than a scribe from whom only 50 lines are available.

The method used in Part III establishes a basis for a comparison between the Italian and French texts, and the comparison of Eighth Century Italian and French variations has therefore been made an integral portion of Part III of this work.

2. The Intensification of the Stress Accent in Northern France

The table which follows summarizes the habits of the French scribes with regard to certain characteristic orthographic substitutions. According to the system already established in Part II, the orthographic variations were divided into those which can be directly connected with the intensification of the stress accent, and those which seem unrelated. The substitution of i for unaccented $\breve{e}$ in hiatus, which seems to us to be a phenomenon particularly characteristic of the intensified stress accent, and for which the scribe of every document has ample opportunity, was considered as a phenomenon apart from the i substitution for unaccented ĕ generally speaking. The orthography i for free accented ē has here been counted with the phenomena not directly connected with intensification of the stress accent; this has been done because the fusion of ĭ, ē>/ę/ can always be considered a sufficient reason for isolated instances of the i for ē orthography, especially since absence or presence of a substitution has been the only criterion for judging the linguistic behavior of each scribe. The choice of this criterion, rather than that of relative frequency of a substitution, has also made it possible, however, to include in this part of the study the original documents written in the period 750-770.[1] While these documents are of course to some extent under the influence of a deliberate orthographic reform, it was hoped that each scribe might use at least once many of those orthographic variants significant of his phonemic pattern.

		STRESS ACCENT PHENOMENA				p>b t>d k>g	NON STRESS ACCENT PHENOMENA									
Period	Scribes	ŏ>u	ĕ>i	ĕ Hiatus>i	i>e		ú>o	í>e	ó[>u	ó]>u	é[>i	é]>i	ŭ>o	ĭ>e	ō>u	ē>i
625-640	5	1	2	-	-	-	-	4	3	3	3	4	4	5	3	1
653-680	11	2	10	10	7	3	1	5	6	5	10	11	10	11	3	8
681-697	14	11	12	12	11	7	4	8	8	9	14	14	14	14	5	12
700-717	8	5	8	8	7	7	2	4	7	6	8	8	8	8	8	7
750-770	7	4	6	4	6	7	2	3	1	4	6	3	5	6	3	4

Figures of above table translated into percentages:

Period																
625-640	100	20	40	-	-	-	-	80	60	60	60	80	80	100	60	20
653-680	"	18	91	91	64	27	9	45	55	45	91	100	91	100	27	73
681-697	"	78	86	86	78	50	29	58	58	64	100	100	100	100	36	86
700-717	"	63	100	100	87	87	25	50	87	75	100	100	100	100	100	87
750-770	"	59	86	59	86	100	29	43	14	59	86	43	72	86	43	59

An examination of the figures on the preceding table reveals that again all the phenomena connected with the intensification of the stress accent show a fairly definite trend to increase during the period. All of them, with the exception of voicing of intervocalic plosives, decrease somewhat during the last period, this general dip in the curve toward increase being apparently due to the factor of partial linguistic or orthographic reform.

As far as the "non stress accent connected" phenomena are concerned, we see that they show the same decrease during the last period--obviously for the same reason. During the first four periods, however, they show no uniform trend toward increase, as do the stress accent connected substitutions. They either stay fairly uniformly on the same level (as for example e for unaccented ĭ), decrease (as o for accented ŭ), or fluctuate erratically (as e for accented ĭ). Thus if they do show a tendency to increase (as for instance i for ē) this tendency may be either only apparent, due to the accident of sampling, or due to a behavior characteristic of ē alone. But there is no overall tendency or principle governing the occurrences of the orthographic variations of the non stress accent phenomena such as there is for those connected with the stress accent.

The behavior of stress accent versus non stress accent phenomena may perhaps be summarized best in the following way: We consider the number of stress accent or non stress accent phenomena within each group as a percentage of the total possible score that the scribes of each period could have achieved and establish a comparison on this basis. The highest possible score equals the number of phenomena multiplied by the number of scribes in the group. In other words, of the 5 scribes of group I, one substituted u for unaccented ŏ, two substituted i for unaccented ĕ, thus giving group I a score of 3, in percentage form 12% of the possible 25 (100%) which group I could theoretically have scored in the stress accent category.

A table summarizing the usages of the scribes within each group according to the above method follows:

	Stress Accent Phenomena		Non Stress Accent Phenomena	
Period	Possible Score	Actual Score	Possible Score	Actual Score
I	25 (100%)	3 (12%)	50 (100%)	30 (60%)
II	55 (100%)	35 (60%)	110 (100%)	70 (64%)
III	70 (100%)	53 (76%)	140 (100%)	102 (73%)
IV	40 (100%)	35 (87%)	80 (100%)	66 (82%)
V	35 (100%)	27 (77%)	70 (100%)	37 (53%)

These results may be graphically presented as follows:

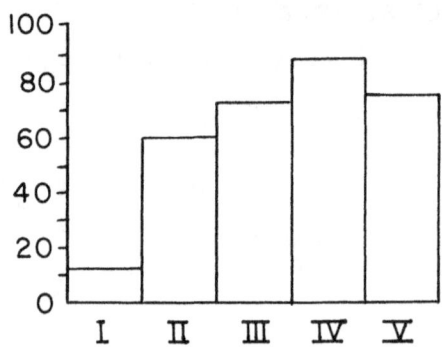 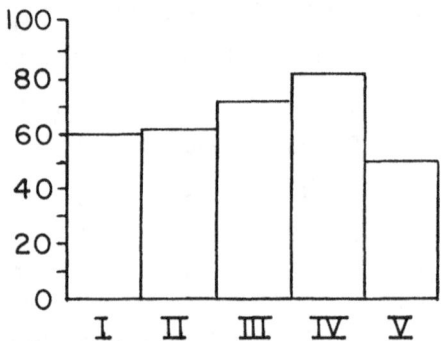

A comparison of the percentage increases in the left and right hand columns of the foregoing table reveals that both stress accent and non stress accent phenomena show throughout the first four periods a tendency to increase. But for the stress accent phenomena this tendency is well marked, especially in the step from the first to the second period. And it is this increase which can be directly associated with the increase in the stress accent during the Seventh Century. Both groups of phenomena also show the decrease in frequency from the fourth to the fifth period apparently caused by a partial orthographic reform. It is of interest to note that this drop in frequency is considerably greater for the non stress accent phenomena, probably indicating an actual increase of the stress accent in the spoken language, and certainly evidence of a greater tenacity of those phenomena representing the actual metamorphosis occurring in the language at that time.

3. Comparison of Habits of 8th Century French and Italian Scribes

In this section the method applied in the preceding section to the French documents alone will be used for a comparative analysis of the Italian and French documents of the 8th Century. The phenomena singled out for tabulation will be for the most part the same that were discussed previously with, however, the following exceptions: unaccented ĕ in hiatus, which hardly ever occurs in the Italian documents, is not included as a separate category in this part of our study; on the other hand, the fall of -t and -s in final position, which Part I showed to be an extremely characteristic feature of the Italian documents, has been included. Furthermore it was thought to be of advantage to include four morphological substitutions which are connected with the fall of final -s: o or u(m) for the nominative -us of the second declension, i or is for the accusative -os of the second declension plural, i for -is of the dative-ablative (or oblique) of the second declension plural, and i for -es of the third declension plural.

A tabulation follows which gives in the first part the actual number of scribes utilizing each phonological variation. The second part of the table repeats the figures of the first in terms of approximate percentages, not including Pisa and Piacenza, however, because the sample of scribes from those areas is relatively small.

	STRESS ACCENT PHENOMENA					NON STRESS ACCENT PHENOMENA								
Area	Scribes*	ŏ>u	ĕ>i	-ĭ>e	p>b t>d k>g	ŭ>o	ĭ>e	ō[>u	ō]>u	ē[>i	ē]>i	ŭ>o	ĭ>e	ō>u	ē>i
Siena	16	4	1	1	-	2	11	11	4	14	10	4	16	8	14
Pisa	7	4	4	2	-	2	2	2	4	7	3	4	2	1	3
Lucca	52	20	19	12	10	23	33	38	20	50	10	42	51	19	24
Piacenza	5	5	5	-	-	2	4	5	1	2	1	5	5	1	2
North. Italy	17	8	7	4	13**	6	15	9	2	8	4	15	17	4	8
North. France	15	9	14	13	14	4	7	8	10	14	11	13	14	11	11

Figures of above table translated into percentages:

Siena	100	25	6	6	-	13	69	69	25	88	63	28	100	50	80
Lucca	"	39	37	23	19	44	63	73	39	94	19	80	98	37	46
North. Italy	"	47	41	23	76	35	88	53	12	46	23	88	100	23	46
North. France	"	60	93	86	93	27	47	53	67	93	73	87	93	73	73

* Only those scribes of whom an actual sample of their handwriting is available have been included here. In addition, one scribe from Northern Italy from whom only a very small sample is available (No. 233) has been omitted. These two factors account for the differences in numbers of scribes as compared with the table given in Part I. (Cf. p. 2 and p. 3).

** This figure does not contradict the statement in Part I, 3.2 that voicing is found in all documents (except one recopied by another scribe) from North of the Po. For in some of the documents the instances of voicing occurred in the statements of the witnesses and not in the portion of the document written by the scribe. These instances have therefore not been included here.

In comparing the figures for the changes directly connected with the stress accent,[2] we note that there is a distinct uniformity among all four phenomena in occurring with maximum frequency in Northern France and minimum frequency in Central Italy, with a definite trend toward gradual decrease from North to South. The conclusion suggested thereby is that Northern France and Northern Italy were areas of intensification of the stress accent, and that in Italy this tendency diminished as it progressed from North to South. Again the phenomena which are not connected with the intensity of the stress accent do not show any such general trend in the frequency of their occurrence.

The table which follows gives the frequency of occurrence of the fall of final -t and final -s and associated morphological phenomena. Percentage figures are given in parentheses.

	Scribes	-s>∅	-t>∅	-us>o	-os>i(s)	-is>i	-es>i
Siena	16	9 (56)	15 (94)	9 (56)	12 (75)	13 (81)	5 (31)
Pisa	7	5	5	5	3	4	2
Lucca	52	18 (35)	45 (86)	39 (75)	23 (44)	32 (62)	11 (21)
Piacenza	5	1	2	2	4	2	-
North. Italy	17	1 (6)	12 (70)	6 (35)	6 (35)	3 (17)	1 (6)
North. France	15	-	-	2 (13)	6 (40)	-	-

The conclusion to be drawn from the above table is a corroboration of the results reached in Part I of this study. The tendency to drop final consonants moved from Central Italy northward and spent itself as it reached the periphery of the area in which it was operative. The figures for the morphological phenomena correlate generally with those for the phonological fall of final -s (Cf. Part I, 3.3).

As in the preceding section we can now summarize the results of our investigation by comparing the scores achieved by the scribes from the six areas in each category of phenomena. Tables and graphs follow:

Stress Accent Connected Phenomena

	100% Score	Actual Score
Siena	64	6 (9%)
Pisa	28	10 (37%)
Lucca	208	61 (29%)
Piacenza	40	11 (25%)
North. Italy	68	32 (47%)
North. France	60	50 (83%)

Fall of Final Consonants

	100% Score	Actual Score
Siena	32	24 (75%)
Pisa	14	10 (72%)
Lucca	104	63 (61%)
Piacenza	20	3 (15%)
North. Italy	34	13 (38%)
North. France	150	-

Fall of Final -s in Noun Morphology*

	100% Score	Actual Score
Siena	48	27 (56%)
Pisa	21	11 (52%)
Lucca	156	82 (52%)
Piacenza	15	4 (27%)
North. Italy	51	10 (20%)
North. France	45	2 (4%)

Non Stress Accent Connected Phenomena

	100% Score	Actual Score
Siena	160	94 (59%)
Pisa	70	35 (50%)
Lucca	520	310 (59%)
Piacenza	50	28 (56%)
North. Italy	170	88 (52%)
North. France	150	103 (68%)

* -os>-is is not included since it does not present a fall of -s.

Again we find Northern France leading with respect to "stress accent connected" phenomena, and in Italy a diminishing of stress accent as one proceeds from North to South. The fall of final consonants and the morphological phenomena related to the fall of final -s show the reverse trend: a decrease in frequency from South to North. The general Romance phenomena show only accidental fluctuation.

CONCLUDING REMARKS

In conclusion we wish to bring out the following points:

1. During the Seventh Century Northern French speech underwent an intensification of stress accent. Since this intensification brought about most of the characteristic features of French Romance, the Seventh Century must be considered as the period during which the most individual characteristics of French speech (fall of final vowels, syncopation, effacement of intervocalic plosives) were determined.

2. The documents show that Italian Romance was decisively influenced by two currents, one an intensification of stress accent which had its maximum power in Northern Italy and which spent itself as it traveled southward, the other the fall of final consonants which evidently originated in Southern or Central Italy and traveled from there toward the North. The meeting of these two currents caused the major dialectal differentiations between Central and Northern Italy. But all evidence seems to indicate that the dialectal borders were not yet established in the Eighth Century. The fact that the two currents just mentioned determined the position of East versus West Romance speech accounts also, it seems, for the position of Sardinian within the East-West Romance picture. For apparently Sardinian, not being affected by either current, keeps final -s, but also shows a minimum effect of stress accent intensification (no early voicing of intervocalic occlusives, full retention of final vowels).

3. The reason for the intensification of the stress accent in Northern France during the Seventh Century, we believe, lies in the influence of Germanic. Although the Franks came into Northern France in the Fifth Century, the full impact of the symbiosis of the two languages did not become apparent until the Seventh Century. The progressively decreasing intensity of the stress accent in Italy from North to South seems also to be in accord with the degree of Germanic influence. For Von Wartburg has demonstrated the diminishing degree of Germanic influence in Italy from North to South historically as well as linguistically.[1] This demonstration of the influence of Germanic upon the development of French Romance gives a different explanation for the origin of the specifically French features than that advanced by Muller.[2] Muller sees the answer in socio-economic developments, and especially in the attempted linguistic reform of Charlemagne, which only emphasized the difference between Latin and the spoken language, and the subsequent recognition in 813 of the spoken language as a tongue independent of Latin. The results of this study, however, seem to indicate that developments distinctive of French Romance antedate by about 150 years the date set by Muller for the emergence of the typically French characteristics, although we do not wish to deny the importance of Charlemagne's reforms for the subsequent development of French Romance.

4. The precise relationship between the spoken and written languages cannot be ascertained, but it cannot be doubted that some connection existed, for there is no other possible explanation for the differences in time and space which appear in the written language. Muller in his Chronology of Vulgar Latin insists on the identity of the spoken and written languages, but steadfastly denies any possibility of the existence of dialectization, and thereby weakens his own point. For while the cohesion within the Roman Empire must have kept dialectal variations to a minimum, it is impossible to believe that in such a vast domain and as late as the 6th or 7th centuries they could have been practically nonexistent; and if the written language does not show any indication of dialectization it cannot be identical with the spoken language. The point we wish to make here, however, is precisely that the documents do show dialectal divergences.

5. We have demonstrated here that dialectal divergences existed in the Romance World as early as the Seventh Century, and we believe that further study will show that they appeared even earlier throughout the Romance world. These divergences may not have been very extensive, however they can be detected by careful quantitative analysis. It is in the nature of linguistics as one of the social sciences that positive evidence can be presented only on the basis of statistical evaluation and quantitative analysis. Therefore it is not enough to show the appearance of specific phenomena in documents of various Romance regions. It is also necessary to show whether these phenomena occur in various regions with significantly different frequencies.[3]

The period preceding the emergence of the Romance languages presents an absorbing and somewhat mysterious problem because of the lack of generally accepted documentary evidence. The chief methods of investigating this period are examination of the internal structural evidence, linguistic geography, reconstruction by the comparative method, and examination of the documentary evidence, and ideally these should go hand in hand. By the use of linguistic geography and the examination of the internal structural evidence relative chronology can be established but not absolute chronology.[4] Reconstruction by the comparative method[5] completely overlooks the essential dimensions of time and space, and is apt to become an exercise unrelated to linguistic reality. By examination of the documentary evidence, however, we can establish absolute chronology, and by the use of statistical counts we can investigate precisely those dimensions of space and time which remain otherwise closed to the scrutiny of the historical linguist.

We do not dispute that many of the linguistic changes discussed in this work, like the fall of -s or the voicing of intervocalic stops, existed in the Romance world in the 2nd or 3rd century. Yet we hope to have demonstrated that it is erroneous to impute to them on the mere basis of their existence for the 2nd and 3rd century a geographic or social extension which they did not reach until many centuries later. The concept of the slow progression of linguistic changes as evidenced by the analysis of Late Latin documents has, for the domain of the Spanish peninsula, been admirably demonstrated by Menéndez-Pidal in his Orígenes.[6] We hope that our study has shown a similar progression of linguistic developments for a few but important features within the 7th and 8th century Northern French and Italian world.

FOOTNOTES

PART I: Introduction

1. Pei, The Language of the Eighth Century Texts in Northern France; Politzer, A Study of the Language of the Eighth Century Lombardic Documents; among other Vulgar Latin studies are Carnoy, Le Latin d' Espagne d' après les inscriptions; Diehl, Vulgär-lateinische Inschriften; Haag, Die Latinität Fredegars; Jennings, A Linguistic Study of the Cartulario de San Vicente de Oviedo; Pirson, La Langue des inscriptions latines de la Gaule; Sas, The Noun Declension System in Merovingian Latin; Schramm, Sprachliches zur Lex Salica; Taylor, The Latinity of the Liber Historiae Francorum; Vielliard, Le Latin des diplômes royaux et chartes privées de l' époque mérovingienne.

2. Politzer, op. cit., Conclusion A.

3. Von Wartburg, Die Ausgliederung der Romanischen Sprachräume; Devoto, La Storia della lingua di Roma.

4. Pei, op. cit., pp. 357-363; Politzer, op.cit., Conclusion B; Haag, op.cit., p. 4. Even those who believe that the difference between spoken and written Latin was considerable are willing to admit that "the vulgar features of the post-classical written language are, of course, derived from vulgar speech", Ernst Pulgram, "Spoken and Written Latin", Language, XXVI (1950), 465.

5. Codice diplomatico longobardo, ed. L. Schiaparelli, Rome, Vol. I, 1929, p. viii, "La nostra raccolta comprende le carte veramente longobarde, scritte in territorio longobardo, durante il regno longobardo."

6. Pei, The Italian Language, p. 155.

7. Pei, op.cit., p. 154.

PART I: Phonology

1. Grandgent, An Introduction to Vulgar Latin, p. 84-86, holds that the fusion of $\breve{i}$ and $\bar{e}$ took place in the Third Century, and that that of $\breve{u}$ and $\bar{o}$ was accomplished by the end of the Fourth Century. Bourciez, Éléments de linguistique romane, p. 42, places the merger of $\bar{e}$ and $\breve{i}$, $\bar{o}$ and $\breve{u}$ in the Third Century.

2. Muller and Taylor, A Chrestomathy of Vulgar Latin, p. 31, explain the orthography i for e as due to the phonetic change $\bar{i}>e$. It is of interest to note, however, that Grandgent, op.cit., p. 83-84, notes that the orthography i was due to the extremely closed pronunciation of the e sound, and that in Southern Italy the final outcome of the Latin $\bar{e}$ was indeed i rather than ę.

3. Long $\bar{o}$ in free position diphthongizes generally in the Gallo-Italian dialects: Latin odore>Gallo-Italian udour (Cf. Pei, The Italian Language, p. 154; Rohlfs, Historische Grammatik der italienischen Sprache I, pp. 142 ff.)

4. Pei, op.cit., p. 154, and Meyer-Lübke and d' Ovidio, Grammatica storica della lingua e dei dialetti italiani, pp. 211-214.

5. Pei, op.cit., p. 36; Grandgent, From Latin to Italian, pp. 41-43, Rohlfs, op.cit. I, p. 216.

6. Grandgent, Introduction to Vulgar Latin, p. 148, is of the opinion that the fourth declension began to be absorbed into the second already in Classical Latin; Bourciez, op.cit., pp. 86-87, states that the transfer of the fourth declension into the second was an early phenomenon. Late retentions of the fourth declension, noted by Rohlfs (op.cit., Vol. II, pp. 32 ff.) are sporadic.

7. The theory advocated by Pei, "Latin and Italian Final Front Vowels", is that i is a possible alternative development of e, as well as the other Latin front vowels, in Italian.

8. This change of $\bar{i}>e$ in the passive infinitive, which interestingly enough occurs also in the Central Italian documents, could of course also be explained as a syntactical phenomenon. Cf. the

discussion concerning the origin of the "faire faire" construction: Muller, Origine et histoire de la préposition "à" dans les locutions du type "faire faire quelque chose à quelqu' un"; Norberg, "Faire faire quelque chose à quelqu' un". Since the confusion of active and passive infinitive takes place in the first, second and fourth conjugations only, a pure phonetic explanation of the i>e change appears more logical. See Politzer, "Far fare qualche cosa". In the same article the suggestion is also made that the confusion of -i and -e may be due to the structural tendency toward symmetry: after the disappearance of the fourth declension, Late Latin had 4 vowel phonemes in the final syllable, o a e i. The loss of the phonemic contrast of e:i restores a symmetrical system, o a e. This tendency to lose the final -i as a distinct phoneme is, however, ultimately counteracted by the fall of final -s, which necessitates the retention of an -i phoneme for morphological reasons (See also Noun Declension, par. 9.6, footnote 11).

9. Pei, The Italian Language, p. 36; Rohlfs, op.cit., p. 219.

10. Simplification of Latin double consonants rather than gemination, and voicing of intervocalic occlusives are chief characteristics of Northern Italian as opposed to Central Italian (Cf. Pei, The Italian Language, pp. 184-185), and at the same time the general features of the Western Romance Dialect group as opposed to the Eastern (for a discussion of this question see Pei, "Intervocalic Occlusives in East and West Romance"). While final consonants of Latin have practically disappeared in present day Northern Italian, the theory of the Spezia-Rimini line presupposes of course that final -s fell in Northern Italy long after it had disappeared from Central Italian. (See Von Wartburg, Die Ausgliederung der romanischen Sprachräume, pp. 27-31.)

11. Cf. footnote 3 of Introduction.

12. Bourciez, op.cit., p. 48, and Grandgent, Introduction to Vulgar Latin, pp. 129-130, seem sure that -m had become silent already in the Classical Latin period.

13. Grandgent, op.cit., p. 120, states that final -t fell first in Southern Italy early in the empire, and during the empire in most of Italy and Dacia.

14. For the theory that -s before its disappearance changed final a or e to i, see Meyer-Lübke and d' Ovidio, Grammatica storica della lingua e dei dialetti italiani, p. 90.

15. Note that retention of -s in verb forms is attested in Venetian texts from the Thirteenth Century (Cf. Pei, The Italian Language, p. 193; Von Wartburg, op.cit., pp. 27-31.)

PART I: Noun Declension

1. Cf. Phonology, footnote 12.

2. The spreading of the -i ending of the genitive of proper names into other functions, and its survival in Old Italian is discussed by Pei in "La Costruzione ' in casa i Frescobaldi' " and "Ab and the Survival of the Latin Genitive in Old Italian".

3. Cf. Phonology, footnote 14.

4. This conclusion coincides with the theory of Dag Norberg who asserts (Syntaktische Forschungen, p. 30) that the tendency to establish -as as sole plural ending existed also in Italy, but that as a result of the fall of final -s, the plural in -e (from -ae) was again restored. An alternative conclusion is suggested by Reichenkron, Beiträge zur romanischen Lautlehre. He explains the Italian plurals in -e as derived from the accusative in -as. The problem faced by this explanation is the existence of feminine plurals in -a not only in the documents, but also in many Italian dialects (Cf. Rohlfs, Historische Grammatik der italienischen Sprache, Vol. II, p. 44 ff.) Reichenkron does suggest differences in the treatment of final -s according to syntactical position and the coexistence of the -a and -e plurals, both derivatives of the -as forms, could then be due to those syntactical variations.

5. Pei, The Italian Language, p. 72.

6. Pei, "Latin and Italian Final Front Vowels".

7. For his own and other scholars' views as to the date of the manuscript, see Schiaparelli, Codice diplomatico longobardo, Vol. I, pp. 236-237.

8. Grandgent, An Introduction to Vulgar Latin, p. 148, accounts for the spelling us for os in the

accusative as an "intermediate confusion" brought about by the analogy with the fourth declension in the process of absorption by the second.

9. This is the theory of Grandgent, who asserts (Introduction to Vulgar Latin, p. 154) that all Romance languages except Spanish modeled their third declension plurals after the second declension, and that this process may have begun before the Seventh Century. Analogy with the second declension is also essentially the explanation accepted by Rohlfs, op.cit., Vol. II, p. 49.

10. Cf. Phonology, footnote 14.

11. Cf. Noun Declension, footnote 5. A theory which mediates between these latter two is advanced by Politzer, "Vulgar Latin -es>Italian -i". In this article it is suggested that in final syllable the /e/ and /i/ phonemes merged to /e/, but that the /e/ phoneme had an allophone /i/ before s. After the fall of -s, this allophone became of morphophonemic value. Reichenkron, op. cit., explains the -i plurals of the third declension as the outcome of the Latin -es forms. Again (Cf. footnote 4, p. 102) one must perhaps fall back on syntactical variation in the treatment of final -s in order to explain the dialectically rather frequent plurals in -e of the type i cane (Rohlfs, op.cit., Vol. II, pp. 49 ff.)

12. This problem is paralleled by the question of the derivation of the -i in second person singular verb forms: Grandgent holds the theory (From Latin to Italian, p. 158-159) that it is due to the analogical influence of the fourth conjugation; Meyer-Lübke and d'Ovidio explain it (Grammatica storica della lingua e dei dialetti italiani, p. 130) by their theory of the closing influence of -s which restricts analogical explanation to the third conjugation; while Pei ("Latin and Italian Final Front Vowels") applies his theory of alternative outcome of final front vowels, reducing the necessity for analogical explanation to the first conjugation. The theory advanced by R. L. Politzer (see footnote 11) is of course also applicable. Examples in the documents of the change -es to -i(s) are few: havis for habes (No. 109), vindici (present subjunctive for vindices) ac defendas (No. 45, 46, 23).

13. For the development of the Latin neuter in Italian, see Pei, The Italian Language, p. 75. For the problem of the confusion of feminine with neuter plurals (le ossa, le capra) see Rohlfs, op.cit., Vol. II, p. 44 ff and pp. 81-82.

PART I: Conclusion

1. Von Wartburg, La Posizione della lingua italiana, p. 13 ff; Die Ausgliederung der romanischen Sprachräume, passim. With regard to the fall of -s, our findings seem to bear out the contention of Rohlfs (op.cit. I, p. 497) that the fall of -s in Italian does not go back to the Vulgar Latin phenomenon and became general only during the Middle Ages.

2. Cf. Introduction, footnote 1.

3. Politzer, A Study of the Language of the Eighth Century Lombardic Documents, tables XVII and XX.

4. Pei, The Language of the Eighth Century Texts in Northern France, Appendix A13 and A15.

5. Politzer, op.cit., table XVIII.

6. Politzer, op.cit., table XIX.

7. Pei, op.cit., Appendix A15.

8. Proskauer, Das auslautende -s auf den lateinischen Inschriften, pp. 30-31 and 81-89 shows that the fall of -s seems to be a phenomenon attested in inscriptions of the entire Romance world. A similar result with regard to syncope is reached by Cross, Syncope and Kindred Phenomena in Latin Inscriptions.

9. This theory was advocated by Politzer, "Final -s in the Romania".

10. Pei, op.cit., Appendix A11, and pp. 75ff., 86ff., 92ff.

11. Pei, op.cit., p. 100.

12. Pei, op.cit., p. 49.

PART II: Introduction

1. Sas, The Noun Declension System in Merovingian Latin. This study shows essentially one thing: the trend toward the establishment of a double case system throughout the Seventh and Eighth

Century Merovingian Latin. In the Eighth Century documents there is a very rudimentary trend to replace the distinct nominative, especially in proper names and place names. See also Pei, The Language of the Eighth Century Texts in Northern France, pp. 214-215, and Politzer, "On the Origin of the Romance Declensional System".

2. Tardif, Monuments historiques, Paris, 1866.

3. See Pei, op.cit., pp. 5-6.

4. Lauer and Samaran, Les Diplômes originaux des mérovingiens, Paris, 1908.

5. See Pei, op.cit., Appendix B.

PART II: Selected Phonological Phenomena

1. For this structural explanation of the /u/ > /ü/ shift, see Haudricourt and Juilland, Essai pour une histoire structurale du phonétisme français, Ch. X. For an argument against the structural explanation and a statement of the Celtic substratum theory see von Wartburg, Die Ausgliederung der romanischen Sprachräume, pp. 36-51.

2. It should be noted, however, that the confusion of active and passive infinitive in Northern France seems to be attested from the Sixth Century, even though the 5 scribes of our Period I keep apart the active and passive infinitives. Examples of confusion of active and passive infinitives are found in the works of Gregory of Tours. Max Bonnet, the outstanding student of the writings of Gregory of Tours, insists that these confusions are original with Gregory and are not due to later copyists (Cf. Muller and Taylor, A Chrestomathy of Vulgar Latin, p. 150, footnote 3.)

3. Two explanations may be suggested: (1) The confusion of -i and -e existed already in the Sixth Century, but the phenomenon was infrequent until the middle of the Seventh Century. (2) The confusion of -i and -e in the Sixth Century was due to the structural trend toward symmetry in the vowel system of the final syllable, while the substitution of e and i in the Seventh Century is due to the general weakening of the vowel in the final syllable, and thus correlated with the stress accent.

4. For this explanation see Martinet, "Occlusives and Affricates with Reference to some Problems of Romance Phonology", p. 121, and Haudricourt and Juilland, op.cit., p. 51. Martinet, "Celtic Lenition and Western Romance Consonants", shows the parallel between the Western Romance shift and the same shift in Celtic. He intimates a substratum influence as responsible for the Western Romance development and thus questions the connection between the Western Romance shift and the stress accent, a connection which has been assumed in this study.

5. See Meyer-Lübke, Historische Grammatik der französischen Sprache, p. 7.

6. Wartburg, Die Ausgliederung der romanischen Sprachräume, pp. 65 ff.

7. Richter, Chronologische Phonetik des Französischen bis zum Ende des 8. Jahrhunderts, p. 7 and p. 15.

8. Wartburg, op.cit., p. 31 and map 10.

9. Richter, op.cit., p. 156.

10. Menéndez Pidal, Orígenes del Español, pp. 241 ff., 256-258. Even though the 11th century Spanish documents may be written in a petrified Latin reflecting popular usages of a period preceding their actual composition (cf. Menéndez Pidal, op.cit., pp. vii-viii), their evidence still precludes any Leonese-Castilian uniformity in voicing of stops during the period itself in which their artificial notarial Latin became petrified. In Menéndez Pidal's opinion the currents of vulgar speech reflected in the documents could perhaps reach back as far as the first centuries of the Medieval period, but certainly not to the 3rd century.

11. See von Wartburg, op.cit., p. 32-33.

12. See Rohlfs, op.cit., I, p. 247.

PART III

1. The documents of the period 750-770 were studied by Pei, The Language of the Eighth Century Texts in Northern France. The statistics and information offered by Pei's study were utilized in

this work and served as a valuable check on the accuracy of our findings.

2. The voicing of intervocalic occlusives and confusion of long i and e in the Central Italian area are compared here with the same phenomena in Northern Italy and Northern France. While it seems legitimate to us to compare them statistically, it should be remembered that structurally the two phenomena are probably not the same in the Central Italian area as they are in Northern Italy and Northern France. The Central Italian instances of voicing may or may not be borrowings from Northern Italy (Cf. Pei "Intervocalic Occlusives in 'East' and 'West' Romance"; von Wartburg, Die Ausgliederung der romanischen Sprachräume, pp. 31 ff.), but are at any rate no indication of the type of structural change (double > single, single unvoiced > voiced, voiced plosive > fricative) of which they form a part in Northern Italy or France. The substitution of e for i in Central Italy may be related to the symmetrization of the vocalic system in the final syllable, rather than to the increased stress accent and progressive weakening of the final vowel. (See Part II, par. 2.5).

CONCLUDING REMARKS

1. Prof. von Wartburg suggests Frankish influence as responsible for most of the characteristic features of French and accounts for many important features of Italian dialects by a Longobard influence which was at its strongest in the Po area and diminished gradually toward the South (Cf. von Wartburg, op.cit., pp. 143-144). Politzer, "On the Romance Third Person Possessives", shows the Germanic influence in the use of the possessive pronoun in the French documents of the Seventh and Eighth Centuries: Germanic sin and iro determine the exclusive use of suus and eorum in Northern France, while Central Italian generalizes suus as the singular as well as the plural possessive.

2. Muller, L' Époque mérovingienne, and A Chronology of Vulgar Latin, especially Chapters X and XI.

3. Thus it has been known for some time from inscriptional evidence that the merger of b and u in initial position was a dialectal feature of Latin characteristic for Southern Italy. See Parodi "Del Passagio di v- in b- e di certe perturbazioni delle legge fonetiche nel latino volgare". For an explanation which connects this dialectal feature of Latin directly with the present Romance dialectal features, see Politzer, "On b and v in Latin and Romance."

4. Haudricourt and Juilland, Essai pour une histoire structurale du phonétisme francais, furnish an excellent example of the combined use of structural and geographical evidence.

5. For a discussion of the reconstruction of early Romance developments with primary emphasis on the comparative method, see R. A. Hall, Jr., "The Reconstruction of Proto-Romance".

6. Cf. Menéndez-Pidal, Orígenes del Español. See especially pp. 533 ff. for his discussion of the nature of linguistic changes.

BIBLIOGRAPHY

Bourciez, E., Éléments de linguistique romane, 4th Ed., Paris, 1946.

Carnoy, A., Le Latin d'Espagne d'après les inscriptions, 2nd Ed., Brussels, 1906.

Cross, Ephraim, Syncope and Kindred Phenomena in Latin Inscriptions, New York, 1930.

Devoto, Giacomo, Storia della lingua di Roma, Bologna, 1940.

Diehl, Ernst, Vulgärlateinische Inschriften, Bonn, 1910.

Grandgent, C. H., An Introduction to Vulgar Latin, Boston, 1907.

Grandgent, C. H., From Latin to Italian, Cambridge, 1933.

Haag, Oscar, Die Latinität Fredegars, Erlangen, 1898.

Hall, Robert A. Jr., "The Reconstruction of Proto-Romance", Language XXVI (1950) 6-27.

Haudricourt, A. G. and Juilland, A. G., Essai pour une histoire structurale du phonétisme francais, Paris, 1949.

Jennings, A. C., A Linguistic Study of the Cartulario de San Vicente de Oviedo, New York, 1940.

Lauer, Ph. and Samaran, Ph., Les Diplômes originaux des mérovingiens, Paris, 1908.

Martinet, André, "Celtic Lenition and Western Romance Consonants", Language XXVIII (1952) 192-218.

Martinet, André, "Occlusives and Affricates with Reference to some Problems of Romance Phonology", Word V (1949) 116-122.

Menéndez-Pidal, R., Orígines del Español (Estado lingüístico de la Península ibérica hasta el siglo XI) 3rd ed., Madrid, 1950.

Meyer-Lübke, Wilhelm, Historische Grammatik der französischen Sprache (2nd and 3rd Ed.), Heidelberg, 1913.

Meyer-Lübke, W. and d'Ovidio, F., Grammatica storica della lingua e dei dialetti italiani, Milano, 1919.

Muller, Henri F., A Chronology of Vulgar Latin, Zeitschrift für romanische Philologie, Beiheft 78, (Halle, 1929).

Muller, Henri F., L'Époque mérovingienne, New York, 1945.

Muller, Henri F., Origine et histoire de la préposition "à" dans les locutions du type "faire faire quelque chose à quelqu'un", Poitiers, 1912.

Muller, Henri F. and Taylor, Pauline, A Chrestomathy of Vulgar Latin, New York, 1932.

Norberg, Dag, "Faire faire quelque chose à quelqu'un", Recherches sur l'origine latine de la construction romane, Sprakvetenskapliga Sällkapets Förhandlinger, Uppsala, 1943-1945, Bilaga E, pp. 65-106.

Norberg, Dag, Syntaktische Forschungen auf dem Gebiete des Spätlateins und des frühen Mittellateins, Uppsala, 1943.

Parodi, E., "Del Passagio di v- in b- e di certe perturbacioni delle legge fonetiche nel latino volgare", Romania XXVII (1898) 177-240.

Pei, Mario A., "Ab and the Survival of the Latin Genitive in Old Italian", Italica XXV (1948) 104-106.

Pei, Mario A., "La Costruzione in casa i Frescobaldi", Lingua Nostra I (1939) 101-103.

Pei, Mario A., "Intervocalic Occlusives in 'East' and 'West' Romance", Romanic Review XXXIV (1943) 235-247.

Pei, Mario A., The Italian Language, New York, 1941.

Pei, Mario A., *The Language of the Eighth Century Texts in Northern France*, New York, 1932.

Pei, Mario A., "Latin and Italian Front Vowels", *Modern Language Notes* LVIII (1943) 116-120.

Pirson, Jules, *La Langue des inscriptions latines de la Gaule*, Bruxelles, 1901.

Politzer, Robert L., "Far fare qualche cosa", *Word* V (1949) 258-261.

Politzer, Robert L., "Final -s in the Romania", *Romanic Review* XXXVIII (1947) 159-166.

Politzer, Robert L., "On the Romance Third Person Possessives", *Word* VIII (1952) 65-71.

Politzer, Robert L., "On b and v in Latin and Romance", *Word* VIII (1952) 211-215.

Politzer, Robert L., "On the Origin of the Romance Declensional System", *Modern Language Notes* LXVI (1951) 145-151.

Politzer, Robert L., *A Study of the Language of the Eighth Century Lombardic Documents*, New York, 1949.

Politzer, Robert L., "Vulgar Latin -es>Italian -i", *Italica* XXVIII (1951) 1-5.

Proskauer, Carola, *Das auslautende -s auf den lateinischen Inschriften*, Strassburg, 1909.

Pulgram, Ernst, "Spoken and Written Latin", *Language* XXVI (1950) 458-466.

Reichenkron, Gunter, *Beiträge zur romanischen Lautlehre*, Jena and Leipzig, 1939.

Richter, Elise, *Beiträge zur Geschichte der Romanismen, Chronologische Phonetik des Französischen bis zum Ende des 8. Jahrhunderts*, Zeitschrift für romanische Philologie, Beiheft 82, (Halle, 1934).

Rohlfs, Gerhard, *Historische Grammatik der italienischen Sprache und ihrer Mundarten*, Vol. I and II, Bern, 1949.

Sas, Louis F., *The Noun Declension System in Merovingian Latin*, Paris, 1937.

Schiaparelli, Luigi, *Codice diplomatico longobardo*, Roma, Vol. I, 1929, Vol. II, 1933.

Schramm, F., *Sprachliches zur Lex Salica*, Marburg, 1911.

Tardif, Jules, *Monuments historiques*, Paris, 1866.

Taylor, Pauline, *The Latinity of the Liber Historiae Francorum*, New York, 1924.

Vielliard, Jeanne, *Le Latin des diplômes royaux et chartes privées de l'époque mérovingienne*, Paris, 1927.

Wartburg, Walther von, *La Posizione della lingua italiana*, Firenze, 1940.

Wartburg, Walther von, *Die Ausgliederung der romanischen Sprachräume*, Bern, 1950.

APPENDIX A

The list of scribes which follows gives first the number assigned the scribe for purposes of reference in Appendix B, then the name of the scribe, the number of the document or documents written by that scribe according to the edition in which it is found (i.e. Tardif for the French and Schiaparelli for the Italian documents), and in parentheses the year of the document. A few of the documents from Northern France have been dated differently according to the Lauer and Samaran edition, and where such differences occur, this date will be included in the parentheses, preceded by the letters LS. The scribes are numbered consecutively throughout, but grouped according to periods (for Northern France) or areas (for Italy) with appropriate headings.

Northern France, Period I, 625-640

1. Syggolenus, No. 4 (625).
2. Ursinus, No. 5 (about 627, LS626).
3. Burgundofaro, No. 6 (628, LS629-39).
4. Dado, No. 7 (631-32, LS631-33).
5. Name unknown, No. 9, (640, LS639-42).

Northern France, Period II, 653-680

6. Beroaldus, No. 11, (653, LS654).
7. Name unknown, No. 12 (about 656, LS639-57).
8. Chrodinus, No. 13 (about 657, LS657-73).
9. Theoberctus, No. 14 (658, LS659).
10. Name unknown, No. 15 (658, LS657-73).
11. Name unknown, No. 16 (658, LS657-73).
12. Name unknown, No. 17 (about 659, LS657-73).
13. Rigobertus, No. 19 (670-671).
14. Droctoaldus, No. 20 (677-78, LS677).
15. Aghiliberthus, No. 21 (677-78, LS677).
16. Odiinberthus, No. 22 (679-80, LS679).

Northern France, Period III, 681-697

17. Rigulfos, No. 23 (about 681, LS673-690).
18. Name unknown, No. 24 (682-83).
19. Vulfolaecus, No. 25 (688-89, LS688); No. 34 (695); LS No. 28 (697).
20. Name unknown, No. 26 (about 690).
21. Abthadus, No. 28 (691).
22. Leudebercthus, No. 29 (about 691).
23. Aghilus, No. 30 (692); No. 31 (692).
24. Chlodoinus, No. 32 (692, LS691).
25. Vualderamnus, No. 33 (693-94, LS693).
26. Sighinus, No. 35 (695).
27. Name unknown, No. 36 (696).
28. Nordeberthus, No. 37 (696).
29. Argobercthus, No. 38 (697).
30. Sicharius, No. 39 (697).

Northern France, Period IV, 700-717

31. Sygobaldus, No. 41 (about 700, LS695-711).
32. Beffa, No. 42 (703).
33. Blatcharius, No. 43 (709).
34. Actulius, No. 44 (710); No. 46 (716); No. 49 (716).
35. Dagobertus, No. 45 (710).

36. Chrodobertus, No. 47 (716).
37. Ermedramnus, No. 48 (716).
38. Raganffridus, No. 50 (717).

Northern France, Period V, 750-770

39. Vuineramnus, No. 53 (750).
40. Name unknown, No. 54 (751).
41. Ejus, No. 55 (753); No. 56 (755); No. 57 (759).
42. Arefredus, No. 59 (766).
43. Hitherius, No. 60 (768); No. 61 (768); No. 62 (768).
44. Agliberthus, No. 67 (769).
45. Firmatus, No. 68 (770).

Italy, Siena (Chiusi, Toscanella)

46. Appo, No. 97 (750).
47. Aboald, No. 174 (763); No. 294 (774).
48. Bonifrid, No. 187 (765).
49. Domnulinus, No. 141 (760); No. 185 (765).
50. Ferucio, No. 213 (768).
51. Firmus, No. 192 (765); No. 248 (770); No. 256 (771).
52. Gausualdu, No. 71 (739).
53. Gaidilapu, No. 97 (746-47).
54. Gauspert, No. 146 (760).
55. Laurentius, No. 104 (752).
56. Maurinu, No. 288 (774).
57. Tachinolfu, No. 55 (736).
58. Trasimundus, No. 263 (772); No. 264 (772).
59. Valdipertus, No. 184 (765).
60. Vuarnegausu, No. 66 (738).
61. Name unknown, No. 57 (735-36).

Italy, Pisa

62. Alpertu, No. 124 (757).
63. Ansolf, No. 23 (720); No. 45 (730); No. 46 (730).
64. Johannis, No. 93 (748).
65. Maccio, No. 183 (765).
66. Roduald, No. 49 (730).
67. Teofrid, No. 98 (750); No. 171 (763).
68. Name unknown, No. 295 (768-74).

Italy, Lucca

69. Achipert, No. 77 (740).
70. Altipert, No. 84 (744-45); No. 87 (746).
71. Austripert, No. 207 (767); No. 219 (768); No. 221 (768); No. 223 (768); No. 232 (769); No. 237 (770); No. 241 (770); No. 244 (770); No. 246 (770); No. 247 (770); No. 256 (771); No. 258 (771); No. 265 (772); No. 276 (772); No. 283 (773).
72. Aut... (illegible), No. 62 (732).
73. Autelmus, No. 144 (760); No. 235 (769); No. 268 (772).
74. Benedictus, No. 292 (774).
75. Chiserat, No. 89 (747); No. 205 (767).
76. Ciacio, No. 58 (736).
77. David, No. 127 (757); No. 138 (759); No. 186 (765); No. 287 (773).
78. Deodaci, No. 56 (736).
79. Deusdona, No. 125 (757); No. 157 (761).
80. Fetro, No. 100 (750).
81. Filippo, No. 242 (770); No. 250 (771); No. 251 (771); No. 255 (771); No. 270 (772); No. 273 (772).

82. Firmiteu, No. 269 (772).
83. Fratellus, No. 139 (759); No. 145 (760); No. 160 (762); No. 166 (762); No. 167 (762).
84. Gaiduin, No. 118 (755).
85. Gaudentius, No. 61 (737); No. 67 (738); No. 73 (740); No. 76 (739-40); No. 94 (748); No. 99 (749-50).
86. Georgius, No. 148 (761); No. 193 (765).
87. Ghisipertu, No. 211 (767).
88. Ghisprand, No. 210 (767).
89. Gunipert, No. 150 (761).
90. Gunprando, No. 280 (773).
91. Lamipert, No. 90 (747); No. 147 (761).
92. Leonacis, No. 42 (728-29).
93. Osprand, No. 108 (753); No. 114 (754); No. 115 (754); No. 120 (755); No. 131 (758); No. 140 (759); No. 149 (761); No. 143 (760); No. 154 (761); No. 156 (761); No. 161 (762); No. 164 (762); No. 165 (762); No. 169 (763); No. 170 (763); No. 175 (764); No. 179 (764); No. 181 (764); No. 182 (764); No. 191 (765); No. 199 (766); No. 202 (766); No. 222 (768); No. 229 (769); No. 238 (770); No. 239 (770); No. 240 (770).
94. Ostripertus, No. 195 (766); No. 197 (766); No. 200 (766).
95. Perterad, No. 85 (746); No. 86 (746).
96. Petrus, No. 69 (739).
*97. Prandulus, No. 136 (759).
*98. Prandulo, No. 178 (764); No. 227 (769).
*99. Prandulus, No. 220 (768); No. 286 (773).
**100. Rachipert, No. 177 (764).
**101. Rachipert, No. 254 (771).
102. Rachiprand, No. 245 (770); No. 259 (772); No. 260 (772); No. 272 (772); No. 279 (773); No. 281 (773); No. 285 (773).
103. Radalpert, No. 102 (752); No. 113 (754); No. 189 (765).
104. Raspert, No. 106 (752); No. 128 (758).
105. Rixsolfus, No. 194 (765).
106. Rotpert, No. 103 (752).
107. Saxu, No. 267 (772).
108. Sicherad, No. 16 (713-14); No. 31 (723).
109. Sichipert, No. 117 (755).
110. Sichiprand, No. 204 (767).
111. Sicoin, No. 34 (724); No. 35 (724).
112. Tanipert, No. 126 (757); No. 133 (759).
113. Teuderado, No. 68 (739).
114. Teudilasco, No. 261 (772).
115. Teutfrid, No. 88,(764).
***116. Teutpert, No. 111 (754).
***117. Teutpert, No. 74 (740); No. 80 (742); No. 91 (747); No. 105 (752); No. 134 (759).
118. Ursu, No. 70 (739).
119. Vuillerad, No. 266 (772).
120. Name unknown, No. 51 (732).

Italy, Piacenza

121. Audoald, No. 291 (774).
122. Ermenfrit, No. 249 (772).
123. Maurace, No. 52 (735); No. 54 (735); No. 59 (736); No. 60 (737); No. 64 (737); No. 79 (742); No. 109 (753); No. 129 (758); No. 159 (762).
124. Peredeo, No. 130 (758).
125. Vitalis, No. 29 (721).

---

*Schiaparelli, Vol. II, pp. 27 and 275, states positively that these are three different individuals, as is obvious from their handwritings.

**These are apparently two different individuals. See Schiaparelli, Vol. II, pp. 143 and 337.

***These are two different individuals. See Schiaparelli, Vol. I, p. 319.

Italy, North of the River Po

126. Alfrit, No. 234 (769).
127. Anspert, No. 119 (754-55).
128. Audo, No. 137 (759).
129. Anstrolf, No. 95 (748).
130. Erminald, No. 190 (765).
131. Faustinus, No. 36 (725).
132. Florentius, No. 216 (768).
133. Garioald, No. 72 (740).
134. Gaff . . . (illegible), No. 284 (773).
135. Lautchis, No. 44 (729).
136. Lazarus, No. 53 (735).
137. Martinus, No. 226 (769).
138. Rimfrit, No. 168 (762).
139. Teoduald, No. 277 (772).
140. Ursus, No. 123 (756).
141. Vualpert, No. 252 (771).
142. Name unknown, No. 81 (721-44).

APPENDIX B

On the following pages examples are given of the most important phenomena--namely the stress accent phenomena and the fall of final -s and -t--considered in the third part of this study, one example for each scribe in whose writing the change occurs. This information will serve as documentation for Part III. Scribes are referred to by the numbers given them in Appendix A, and the document number is given parenthetically only where the scribe has written more than one document.

Short unaccented ĕ>i:

Northern France, Period I: 2. confirmari (active infinitive) deberemus; 3. noluemus denegari.

Northern France, Period II: 6. oportit; 7. confermassit; 8. debirint; 9. ordini; 10. parti; 11. possidit; 12. deberint; 13. facire; 15. debirit; 16. tenuissint.

Northern France, Period III: 17. proficire; 19. oportit (25); 21. voluntati (ablative); 22. quislibit; 23. conponire (30); 24. dicirit; 25. contradixissit; 26. ficissit; 27. inlexerit; 28. constituissit; 29. de parti; 30. licit.

Northern France, Period IV: 31. qualibit; 32. obponire; 33. conparassit; 34. fistivitate (44); 35. fuissit; 36. tilenariis; 37. fuissit; 38. maiorim.

Northern France, Period V: 39. gregim; 40. residissit; 41. diniare; 42. sibi (for sive); 43. quietim (61); 44. facire.

Italy, Siena
51. conpetire (248).

Italy, Pisa
62. pro temporit; 63. qualivit (45); 64. lavorari (as active infinitive); 65. qualivit.

Italy, Lucca
71. iuberis (283); 73. minuire (144); 77. ego ipsi (287); 78. quatinus; 85. debuissim (61); 91. debiris (147); 92. referri (active infinitive); 93. pertenit (239); 99. ipsi (for ipse - 220); 100. ipsi (for ipse); 101. consintire; 102. iuberis (272); 103. illi (for ille - 102); 106. donari et offerri (active infinitive); 108. admonit (16); 110. ipsi (for ipse); 111. extrinsico (34); 112. ipsi (for ipse - 133); 117. tricenti (105).

Italy, Piacenza
121. quatinus; 122. tinore; 123. havit (60); 124. accepissit; 125. genetricim.

Italy, North of the River Po
126. tenit; 128. essit; 130. habit; 131. advenessit; 133. devit; 137. contenit; 142. Campelliuni.

Short unaccented ĕ>i in hiatus

Northern France, Period I: no examples

Northern France, Period II: 6. liciat; 7. puciatur; 8. idio; 9. habiant; 10. habiat; 11. debiat; 13. tinia; 14. dibiat; 15. postia; 16. abiat.

Northern France, Period III: 17. valiat; 19. postia (25); 21. dibiat; 22. habiat; 23. olio (30); 24. habiant; 25. studiat; 26. habiat; 27. liciat; 28. debiat; 29. habiat; 30. possediat.

Northern France, Period IV: 31. antia; 32. viniis; 33. habiat; 34. posthia (44); 35. posthia; 36. habiant; 37. dibiad; 38. antia.

Northern France, Period V: propteria; 40. vinias; 44. tenias; 45. spontania.

Unaccented short ŏ>u

Northern France, Period I: 4. Diunensi.

Northern France, Period II: 7. bunuaria; 8. tempure.

Northern France, Period III: 17. custus; 19. creatur (for creator - 34); 20. cummutavi; 21. antecessur; 22. bunuaria; 23. corpure (30); 24. autur; 25. genitur; 26. genetur; 28. Diunisiae; 30. bunuaria.

Northern France, Period IV: 34. tempure (46); 35. auditur (for auditor); 36. corpure; 37. tempure; 38. custus.

Northern France, Period V: Curborio; 40. Diunissi; 42. Dyunisia; 45. Funtanas.

Italy, Siena
46. cunvinet; 48. purecta; 49. purecta; 59. cummutandi.

Italy, Pisa
62. Langubardorum; 63. diacunu (45); 64. diacunus; 66. cumplevi.

Italy, Lucca
73. diacunus (144); 77. devulvantur (127); 78. udierna; 81. cummanetis (242); 85. cunquisitionem (61); 86. udierna (193); 87. sacerdus; 88. munitario; 89. cunquirere; 92. cunquisito; 93. Ruselle; 94. habitatur (for habitator - 197); 95. cunpuna (86); 96. cunparationem; 102. munitario (281); 107. costus; 108. cummendare (16); 111. cunparavimus (34); 112. creatur (for creator - 126); 117. cunponere (74).

Italy, Piacenza
121. rectur; 122. cummutari; 123. scriptur (54); 124. scriptur; 125. genitur.

Italy, North of the River Po
126. custus; 127. meliurada; 130. donatur (for donator); 132. uriente; 134. judicatur (for judicator); 135. cumplivit; 138. genitur (for genitor); 141. scriptur.

Long $\bar{I}$>e in final syllable

Northern France, Period I: No examples

Northern France, Period II: 6. vise (masc. plural); 8. eam ... decrivemus adfirmare; 10. Chlodovie (genitive); 13. monastirium ... decrivi fundare; 14. eam ... decrivemus roborare; 15. vise (masc. plural); 16. capella domni Martine.

Northern France, Period III: 17. ipsius monastirie; 19. predicti monastiriae (25); 20. sepulturoli meae; 22. fiere; 23. vise (masc. plural); 24. fiere; 25. quod dici aut nomenare potest; 26. heredis suae; 27. tribunal aeterne iudicis; 28. ipsius monastiriae; 29. monasthirie sui.

Northern France, Period IV: 31. eam decrivemus adfirmare; 32. ipsius monastyriae; 33. vindicione ... adfirmare rogassit; 34. predicte monastyriae (44); 35. vise (masc. plural); 36. misse (masc. plural); 38. eam dicrevimus roborare.

Northern France, Period V: 39. vicecomete palate nostro; 40. quod ... nomenare non fuit necessarium; 41. ille monachy dicebant (55); 43. divine nominis (61); 44. ad bonis hominebus adfirmare rogavimus; 45. quam ... adfirmare rogavimus.

Italy, Siena
57. minare (active infinitive).

Italy, Pisa
64. de ipsi diacones; 65. fiere.

Italy, Lucca
74. fiere; 77. futures temporibus (127); 81. firmare te prevideo (273); 83. minare (139); 85. monusculi nostre (67); 93. menare (238); 102. me rectorem ... ordinare iuberis (272); 103. demandavet ... cartula relevare (102); 104. cartula ... fecimus ... exemplare (128); 105. me dominus ... vocare iussere; 112. fiere (126); 113. fiere.

Italy, Piacenza: no examples

Italy, North of the River Po
126. quod ... conservare promitto; 131. promettit ... ipso puero ... defensare; 133. fiere; 136. fiaere.

Voicing of Intervocalic Occlusives

Northern France, Period I: no examples

Northern France, Period II: 8. podibat; 13. adebisci; 16. segundo.

Northern France, Period III: 17. redebicione; 19. vogatur; (LS28); 20. audentico; 21. noncobantis; 22. vindegare; 24. vindegatas; 18. estibulacione.

Northern France, Period IV: 31. Parisiago; 32. repeditione; 33. elidigatas; 34. plagabile (46); 35. elidiatum; 36. rodatico; 37. elidiata.

Northern France, Period V: 39. fistugo; 40. evindegatas; 41. Parisiago (55); 42. Habriciago; 43. Propiniagas (62); 44. conplaguit; 45. istibulatione.

Italy, Siena: no example

Italy, Pisa: no example

Italy, Lucca
71. viganium (241); 77. exeguta (138); 83. viganio (160); 85. memedipsum (61); 93. viganeo (164); 101. viganium; 103. viganeum (113); 107. viganeum; 117. negudiante (80); 120. genetrige.

Italy, Piacenza: no examples

Italy, North of the River Po
126. hedernam (for aeternam); 127. terredurio; 129. prado; 130. repeditione; 131. dogomentum; 133. sebe (for saepe); 134. suberius; 135. predegationem; 136. pedidus; 138. pegunia; 140. olivedo; 141. vigo; 142. precibimus.

Fall of final -t

Italy, Siena
46. aliquis homo vineris; 47. pos (294); 49. capo (141); 50. pos; 51. pos (192); 52. dica; 53. habe; 54. curre; 55. qualive; 56. constans (for constat); 57. fueri; 58. consta (263); 59. consta; 60. constans; 61. divea.

Italy, Pisa
63. convine (45); 65. pos; 66. qualive; 67. sia (171); 68. confirmave.

Italy, Lucca
69. habeas et possedeas ipse sanctus locus; 70. fia (84); 71. posse (for posset - 207); 73. consa (for constat - 268); 74. res mea ... pertenerem deveas; 75. pos; 76. rogavi (for rogavit); 77. nullus ... haveas potestatem (138); 78. pos; 79. tene (125); 80. oporte; 81. posse (for possit - 252); 82. conpona; 83. pos; 84. fuere (for fuerit); 85. incurra (61); 86. fuere (148); 87. tene; 88. consta; 89. possa; 90. reside; 92. pos; 93. posse (for possit -114); 94. posset (195); 95. colive (86); 96. qualive; 97. fueri; 98. tene (227); 99. capo; 100. consta; 101. tene; 102. posse (245); 103. fuera (113); 104. tene (106); 105. iussere; 107. tene; 108. abse (for absit); 109. pos; 112. presumsere (for presumpserit - 126); 113. manea; 114. fuere; 115. decorre; 116. manea; 117. pos (80); 120. offerse (for offersit).

Italy, Piacenza
121. da; 123. valueri.

Italy, North of the River Po
127. tene; 129. pos; 130. confer (for confert); 132. pos; 133. fuere; 134. consta; 135. pos; 136. duxe; 139. placuere; 140. quesiere; 141. pos; 142. savere (for saperet).

*Fall of final -s

Italy, Siena
46. sumu; 49. manibu; 52. credimu; 53. promittimu; 54. subtu; 56. subtu; 58. fuerimu; 60. bu (for vos); 61. tu . . . paraveri.

Italy, Pisa
63. vindici (for vindices - 23); 64. signum manu; 67. os anno (for hos annos - 98); 68. omnes adquisito; 62. manibus sui.

Italy, Lucca
70. heredi meus (87); 73. quesierimu (44); 78. civis Lucensi; 84. tu . . . devea; 85. ipso suprascripto soledo dante vidi (in reference to a plural - 61); 90. fori (for foris); 93. fore (for foris - 114); 95. in ipsa calendas (85); 98. superiu; 99. ipsas re mea quas tibi dare videor (286); 101. mino; 108. novi (for nobis - 31); 110. manibus mei; 113. tre; 114. alia omnes res meas; 117. de posteros tuo (80); 120. ad alia vine nostra; 83. duas pagina (139).

Italy, Piacenza
124. curtivo (for cortivus).

Italy, North of the River Po
136. Kalendas februaria.

---

* The reader is reminded that under "Fall of final -s" we have tried to isolate instances of fall of -s which can be considered as purely phonological. Thus, any fall of -s which can be interpreted as the substitution of another case ending of the same number and the same declension has not been counted. E.g.-a for -as in the feminine plural was included, but -i for -is in the masculine plural was not. -i for -es in the plural of the 3rd declension, which was considered as a separate category, was also not included in the count.

APPENDIX C

This portion of the appendix has been included for two important reasons: first, to give the reader a clearer idea of the sort of language the documents are written in, and the system of analysis employed; second, to supplement the examples quoted out of context throughout the work by analyzing a few connected passages.

The passages were chosen at random, and include four selections from the documents of Italy, and two from the material from Northern France. The phenomena occurring in each passage were classified according to the number of the paragraph in which the specific phenomenon is discussed, and listed by those numbers, reference always being made to Part I for the Italian documents, and Part II for the French.

Lines 14-20, Document 66 (Siena), <u>Codice paleografico longobardo</u>, Vol. I, p. 207.

"... et suscipemus nus q(ui) s(upra) bindi/toris ad bu s(upra)s(crip)ti emtoris pro ipsa s(upra)s(crip)-ta/ terras c(um) homnias q(ue) s(upra) positas abes integro/ pretius auri soledus hobridiacus pensantis/ numerus duo et .II. trimissi adfenitus;/ quatenus hab h(odierna) d(ie) abeatis, teneatis, posse/-deatis, bel, si binderes aut dunares bolueritis/ liberas in omnebus habeatis potestatem."

1.2 $\acute{\bar{e}}[>$i: suscipemus (for suscepimus)

   $\acute{\bar{e}}]>$i: binderes

1.3 $\acute{\bar{o}}>$u: nus (for nos), bu (for vos)

2.1 $\bar{e}>$i: binditoris

   $\breve{i}>$e: suscipemus, soledus, possedeatis, omnebus

2.2 $\bar{o}>$u: dunares

2.4 $\breve{e}>$i: trimissi (for tremisses)

2.5 $\breve{i}>$e: adfenitus

3.3 fall of -s: bu (note that following word begins with s-)
   addition of -s: abes (for habet), binderes, dunares, liberas (for liberam)

5.4 2nd Decl. Acc. Sing.: integro pretius (for integrum pretium)

5.5 2nd Decl. Abl. Sing.: numerus duo

7.4 1st Decl. Abl. Pl.: pro ipsa suprascripta terras

8.4 2nd Decl. Acc. Pl.: soledus, adfenitus

8.5 2nd Decl. Abl. Pl.: suprascripti

9.1 3rd Decl. Nom. Pl.: binditoris (for venditores)

9.4 3rd Decl. Acc. Pl.: pensantis, trimissi

9.5 3rd Decl. Abl. Pl.: emtoris

10.1 2nd Decl. Neuter Pl.: suprapositas

10.2 3rd Decl. Neuter Pl.: (cum) homnias

Note: "cum homnias suprapositas abes" is a typical Vulgar Latin construction; cf. French "il y a".

Lines 3-5, Document 102 (Lucca), <u>Codice paleografico longobardo</u>, Vol. I, p. 295.

"... Constat me [Uuille]/rad cl(ericum) filio q(uon)d(am) Iffuloni uendedisset et uendedi, trad[edisset]/ et tradedi tibi Crespino duo petzioli de prato et uno de terr̥ [a]/ lauoraturia ..."

1.3 ó>u: lauoraturia

2.1 í>e: uendedisset, uendedi, tradedi, Crespino

3.3 addition of -t: uendedisset

5.4 2nd Decl. Acc. Sing.: filio

5.64 2nd Decl. Acc. Proper Name: Uuillerad

6.6 3rd Decl. Gen. Proper Name: Iffuloni

8.4 2nd Decl. Acc. Pl.: duo petzioli

Lines 11-14, Document 106 (Lucca), <u>Codice paleografico longobardo</u>, Vol. I, p. 304.

". . . ispondeo me ego q(ui) s(upra) Uuilleradu cliricho una cum meus eridis tiui Crispino / uel at tui heridi ispondeo me esset conponiturus duplas tales terra,/ sub istimationem qualis ta fuere . . ."

1.2 é>i: cliricho, eridis, heridi

2.1 í>e: fuere (for fuerint)

2.7 Prothesis: ispondeo, istimationem (this is considered as prothesis because the form "stimatione" occurs quite frequently--it might also, of course, be considered a vowel change, ae>e>i.)

3.3 fall of -t: fuere (for fuerint)
addition of -t: esset

5.4 2nd Decl. Acc. Sing.: cliricho

5.64 2nd Decl. Acc. Proper Name: Uuilleradu

6.5 3rd Decl. Abl. Sing.: istimationem

7.3 1st Decl. Acc. Pl.: duplas terra

8.4 2nd Decl. Acc. Pl.: tui, conponiturus (possibly singular)

8.5 2nd Decl. Abl. Pl.: meus

9.1 3rd Decl. Nom. Pl.: qualis

9.4 3rd Decl. Acc. Pl.: heridi, tales

9.5 3rd Decl. Abl. Pl.: eridis

Lines 2-6, Document 284 (Bergamo), <u>Codice paleografico longobardo</u>, Vol. II, p. 411.

". . . Consta nos Agep(er)t cl(ericus) seo et Gaifrit germanis, habidadoris in uico Castell [is]/ et mundiadoris accepissimus et in presentia testib(us) accepimus ad te Anso[a]l[do]/ filio b(one) m(emorie) Albinoni et mundiadore nostro auri tremissis duos . . ."

1.2 é>i: accepissimus

3.2 voicing of intervocalic occlusive: habidadoris, mundiadoris, mundiadore

3.3 fall of final -t: consta

5.61 2nd Decl. Nom. Proper Names: Agepert, Gaifrit

6.6 3rd Decl. Gen. Proper Name: Albinoni

8.1 2nd Decl. Nom. Pl.: germanis

9.1 3rd Decl. Nom. Pl.: habidadoris, mundiadoris

9.2 3rd Decl. Gen. Pl.: testibus

9.4 3rd Decl. Acc. Pl.: tremissis

* * *

Note: In the excerpts from the French documents, which follow, superscript numbers refer to lines in the text.

Document No. 11, <u>Monuments historiques</u>, p. 10.

"... quia nos, pro Dei amore vel pro reverencia ipsorum sanctorum marterum et adhepiscenda vita aeterna, hunc beneficium ad locum sanctum cum consilio pontefecum et inlustrium virorum[10] nostrorum procerum, gra(tiss)emo anemo et integra volontate vise fuemus pr(esteti)sse, eo scilecit ordene ut si(cut temp)ore (domni) et genetoris nostri ibidem psallencius (per t)urmas fuit instetutus, vel sicut a(d monas)t(hir)ium Sancti Maurici Agaunis die noctoque tenetur, ita in loco ipso celebretur. Quam viro autoretate decrivemus, Christum in omnebus nobis subfragantem, ut fir-[11] mior habeatur, et per tempora conservitur, subscripcionebus man(us nostrae) infra roborare. Beroaldus optulit."

1.1 ē>i: viro, decrivemus, conservitur

  ĭ>e: pontefecum

2.1 ĭ>e: marterum, pontefecum, gratissemo anemo, fuemus, scilecit, ordene, genetoris, instetutus, autoretate, decrivemus, omnebus, subscripcionebus.

2.2 ŭ>o: volontate

2.3 ĕ>i: scilecit

2.5 -ī>e: vise, autoretate decrivemus . . . roborare

Document No. 42, <u>Monuments historiques</u>, p. 35.

(9) "... Proinde, nos taliter, una cum nostris procerebus, constetit decrivrisse, ut dum inluster vir Ghyslemarus, comes palati nostri, testimoniavit, et inter ipsis fuit judicatum, ut dum contra ipsa strumenta nihil habebat[10] quod dicere nec quod obponeret, per sua festuca se exinde in presenti dixit, esse exitum, jobemus ut ipso monasthyriolo superius nomenato Lemauso, cum omni integritate sua, ad se pertenente vel aspiciente, quem[11] iam dictus Gammo condam vel conjox sua Adalgudis, per eorum strumenta, ad ipso monasthyrio Sancti Vincenti vel domni Germani condonarunt vel quicquid ipso Gammo moriens dereliquit, abisque repedicione[12] jamdicta Adalgude aut heredibus suis, omni tempore, ad partem ipsius monasthyriae Sancti Vincinti vel domni Germani, aut rectoris suos, habiant aevidicatum adque aelidiatum: et sit inter ipsis ex hac re[13] in postmodo subita causacio. Beffa recognovit ac subscribsit.

[14] Datum quod ficit minsis Februarius dies XXV, anno VIII rigni nostri, Carraciaco feliciter."

1.1 ē>i: ficit, minsis, rigni, monasthyriolo

2.1 ē>i: decrivisse

  ĭ>e: procerebus, nomenato, pertenente, aevidecatum

2.2 ō>u: subita (for sopita)

  ŭ>o: jobemus, conjox, monasthyriolo

2.3 ĕ>i: ipsi (for ipse)

  ĕ in hiatus>i: habiant

2.5 -ī>e: monasthyriae

3.1 Voicing of intervocalic occlusives: repedicione, aelidiatum, subita

The Department of Romance Studies Digital Arts and Collaboration Lab at the University of North Carolina at Chapel Hill is proud to support the digitization of the North Carolina Studies in the Romance Languages and Literatures series.

www.ingramcontent.com/pod-product-compliance
Lightning Source LLC
Chambersburg PA
CBHW080637230426
43663CB00016B/2906